CREATIVE SAND ART

CREATIVE SAND ART

by R. Thom House

GROSSET & DUNLAP
A FILMWAYS COMPANY
Publishers • New York

Created by: R. Thom House
Photography: John M. Kolego
Sand Paintings: Jeanne Ackerman
                  Ann Ceglia
Illustrations: Barbara Garbutt
                  Bruce A. Genther

A special thanks to Mary L. Griffin, without whose
help this book would not have been possible.

CONTENTS

I
HISTORY

Sand painting as we know it today has evolved over a period of the past several hundred years. The basic concept of layering colored material, be it ground glass, rock or sand, into containers has literally traveled around the world.

In the 1770's news of the craft traveled by word of mouth between tribes of American Indians, namely the Sioux and Choctaw, who were layering local, naturally colored sand into small bottles to sell for profit to passing tourists. The design schemes were of a geometric nature, close copies of the blanket patterns woven by the Indian women.

Strangely enough this same practice was very much in evidence at that same time in some South American countries. Since the distance between these two cultural areas was so great it seems highly unlikely that ideas were exchanged. The only influencing factor that could have nurtured two very separate groups into producing such similar art work was the availability of naturally colored aggregates in each geological area.

The Indians of North America were, in some cases, surrounded by the desert, where an abundance of beautifully colored sands was a natural phenomenon. By the same token the natives of Brazil, where the majority of this type of art was done and is still in evidence today, have at their disposal a wealth of earth and rock rich in mineral content. The minerals themselves are largely responsible for the coloration of the mountain rocks. After grinding, these rocks provide an excellent medium with which to render sand (in this case ground rock) designs. Since the materials used in these examples of sand art are of natural origin, the shades tend to be earthy and subdued.

This type of sand art is not to be confused with the traditional Indian sand painting done in connection with religious ceremonies. Those symbolic sand designs are done on a smooth area of ground or on a piece of animal skin and must be destroyed before sundown so as not to anger the spirits. Each "painting" has a special interpretation befitting a specific situation; i.e., harvest time or the coming of spring; or they can be created as a tribute to any of the many Indian gods. It is interesting to note that these renditions are never done within a container, for this would constitute sacrilege.

It was not until 1855 that a form of sand painting again emerged on the art scene. This variation was a hobby-oriented craft and was soon all the rage in Europe. Ladies from all parts of Europe, most notably Paris, were soon enthusiastically gluing ground glass inside large-mouthed glass canisters to form pleasing design schemes. The craft was originally developed as a method whereby those interested could create for themselves a facsimile of popular Chinese porcelain vases that were, as they are now, too expensive for most households. The designs, most of them copied from the real McCoy, were surprisingly accurate. The art was called potichomani. Later in the 19th century, around 1880, the craft evolved into a closer replica of our present-day sand painting, with the use of rock sand in place of the ground glass. These containers with their glued-in designs were then filled with flour or a similar material and "planted" with dried flowers or fronds of asparagus fern. This was the first known combination of a sand design with a planting for decorative purposes and was definitely the forerunner of our sand-painted terrariums.

In 1882 Mr. A. Clemens, a deaf-mute, fashioned some remarkable sand renditions. His most notable works, the Lord's Prayer and a Mississippi Steamboat, both done entirely in sand, have been purchased by a collector in Massachusetts. Unfortunately for Mr. Clemens, he did not live to receive the recognition and fame deserved for such meticulous work. He sold his art as a means of support, but probably did not personally realize the true value of his works. He died in his home town of McGregor, Iowa, and his remarkable talent was not recognized until after his death.

Sometime in the 20th century, sand art again appeared as a profitable craft, for Israeli artists. It seems that, again, locally available natural materials prompted the craftsmen to take advantage of an increasing tourist trade. Stimulated by a renewed religious awareness, many people were making a pilgrimage to the cradle of ancient religious beliefs. The techniques were kept a secret, which aroused much curiosity and perhaps led the way to what was to take place in America in the following years.

In the United States during the 1920's, a form of terrariums had taken root in the American heart. Called Chinese Gardens, they were simple containers planted with moss and small plants bearing red berries. This was the American version of the European Wardian case. It was not until the early 70's that another "Green Revolution" swept the country. A new interest in greenery led to the terrarium craze that had harried retailers trying to cope with glassware shortages. Almost anything that was transparent became a potential terrarium. The time was ripe for colored sand to be incorporated into terrarium building. Since sand provided excellent drainage in any container and also acts as a reservoir for excess moisture to be drawn up by the plants as needed, it seemed logical that sand design be incorporated into terrarium building.

Thus, inspiration came from the conglomerate ideas of many individuals over several hundred years, the fruits of which have provided us with an interesting, entertaining, and challenging hobby craft today.

II FUNDAMENTAL RULES

Sand art is an interesting and rewarding pastime for anyone, young or old. Fascination is generated as progressive lessons become more complex. Initial lessons, however, should make apparent one very important point—the techniques employed, rather than one's artistic abilities, determine the quality of the end result. Remember that skill in maneuvering the sand into place will increase with practice, as will the quality of the design. It is important to mention at this point that one of the things to keep in mind for good sand designing is to first RELAX! If any mistakes occur, they are easily corrected with the flick of an artist's brush. Sand that has been spooned into the container is easily maneuvered into position, or removed if necessary from the side of the glass to the center area, where it will not show. Approach new design patterns with confidence. The attitude taken is closely linked with success or failure. As we develop our skills in the following chapters, it should be obvious that the natural flow of sand will, in most cases, create the intended design as it is poured from a bent teaspoon with little manual maneuvering by the designer.

There are three basic principles in sand painting that we shall demonstrate here as important preliminary exercises and as an introduction to the ways of sand. These fundamental techniques are layering, poking, and mounding.

INSTRUMENTS

Before we elaborate further on the actual techniques needed to execute some basic designs, it will first be necessary to review the tools needed to sand paint. All of these instruments can usually be found around the house. If you would rather start by purchasing them, it should be noted that your initial investment will be minimal.

1. An iced-tea spoon bent to about a fifty-degree angle for spooning sand.

2. An upholstery needle (or other long instrument with a sharp point).

3. Knitting needles of various sizes (numbers one and five are the most necessary).

4. Artist's brushes for shaping sand and for moving unwanted sand from the side of the container to the center area when correcting designs.

5. Empty cups to mix colors and to hold the different colored sands for accessibility.

6. A turntable or lazy Susan to enable you to more easily move the container as you create your sand design.

7. Any interesting, clear (preferably glass) container.

8. Many and various shades of microfine colored sand. (NOTE: the author highly recommends the use of Terrasand, Sandman, or Sand Pallet, fine quality sands available in many colors and package sizes for your convenience. In addition, they are guaranteed colorfast and nontoxic to insure the longevity of your finished design as well as the health of the plants in the container. Use care when you choose the sand that you will work with. It is critical that a good quality sand be used. Some of the colored sands presently available tend to be of a grainy nature. These types will not allow you to achieve the detail and fine lines necessary for quality designs. On the other hand there are some types of sand that are extra fine. This too is undesirable in that the sand tends to be powdery and will stick

to the sides of the container, or worse yet, will produce blurry designs.)

Before we execute the three basic techniques mentioned earlier, there are some primary guidelines that need to be clarified.

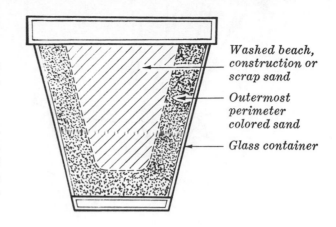

Washed beach, construction or scrap sand

Outermost perimeter colored sand

Glass container

Sand should always be poured against the wall of the container. This will concentrate the colored sand in the actual design area, the outermost perimeter of the container's area. It would be wasteful and expensive to fill the entire container with colored sand. As you follow these directions, you will notice that a hollow area will be created in the center region. Fill this depression with washed beach sand (the salt residue on natural beach sand will cause harm to the plants) or construction sand. Construction sand can be purchased at most garden centers and is fairly inexpensive. Perhaps best of all would be to use scrap sand, mixed up colors of sand used for a previous design that was unsatisfactory for one reason or another. By following this suggestion there will be no waste of colored sand at all!

When each design is completed, it is advisable to top the finished sand painting with a layer of black sand. This layer will serve as a liner between the design and the soil that will be used for planting. Obviously, soil is of a different texture than the finer sand material. If the soil were placed directly over the sand painting, an uneven top would result when the soil was packed into place. A neat, finished look is as important as the quality of the design itself. Apply this black sand liner as soon as the design is completed; this will also prevent the design from shifting when the soil mixture is tamped into place.

Soil mixture

Charcoal

Black sand liner

Completed sand design.

Perhaps a word about correct soil mixture should be mentioned at this time. The most successful terrariums employ a mixture of two parts potting soil, one part peat moss, one part pearlite or vermiculite, and, if desired, one-half part charcoal mixed throughout the soil. You may, of course, place the charcoal in a layer over the black sand liner and then tamp the soil over all. The charcoal, however, does very well as a soil sweetener when blended with the planting mixture. It is not necessary for the charcoal to be a separate layer. (Example: two cups soil, one cup peat moss, one cup pearlite or vermiculite with one-half cup charcoal mixed in.)

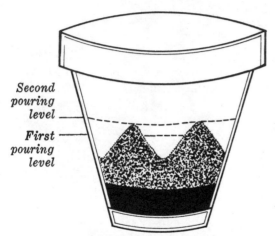

Movement of spoon illustrating center to edge pouring motion.

Second pouring level

First pouring level

Technique employed in covering mountains in levels.

Cover existing forms from behind to prevent slippage.

PRIMARY EXERCISES

Mentioned earlier was the necessity of pouring the sand against the glass. There is a knack to pouring sand in this manner that will become second nature after some practice. The illustration should make clear the motion of pouring from center to edge.

By following this technique you will also be learning a very important skill and basic rule. Whenever you are placing a layer of sand on an existing shape or form (i.e., hills, mountains, birds, etc.) always approach the pouring aspect with this "center to edge" motion in mind. Cover birds from behind, center to edge, so that the added weight of the sand over the shape will not flatten what you have already built. For example, fill the valleys between mountains or hills first; then, in stages, cover the peaks completely. By starting from the lowest levels, then building up and covering the upper levels of forms, you can prevent slippage of any sand. Support the existing forms with background as the design progresses—this is the key to remember.

With these fundamental pouring rules in mind and the basic tools assembled you can now continue to build upon your knowledge by trying the three initial and primary techniques. Remember also, as you begin, that errors can be corrected very easily by using the artist's brush.

Since this sand art is for practice only, and will most likely not be used for a terrarium, plan to save the sand as scrap for filler later on. The same container can be used for all of the exercises.

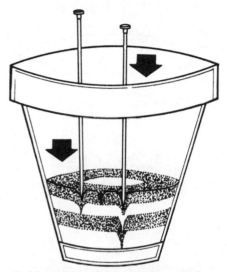

Center area with filler sand.
Even layers of different colors
(note: they may be of any depth).

Layering

Layering is the simple process of spooning sand into the container. Different colors may be placed around the container, against the inside wall, in equal or varied depths; spoon filler sand into the center as you progress.

Poking

Now that the layers are in place, it would seem logical to next learn about poking through the layers to achieve a design.

Hold a knitting needle against the inside glass container wall. With a definite deliberate stroke, poke down. Remove the needle by first pulling it back towards the center of the container and then completely out of the sand. After repeating this procedure several times, you will see a pattern forming. Try poking down only halfway, or through only two or three layers for variation, remembering each time to pull the needle back and then out of the sand.

By employing this poking technique, you may make birds, sailboats, flowers, and any number of geometric designs.

Poking through layers alternately.

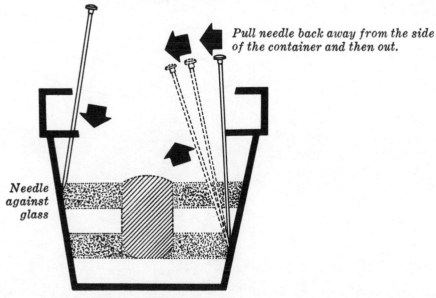

Pull needle back away from the side of the container and then out.

Needle against glass

CROSS SECTION

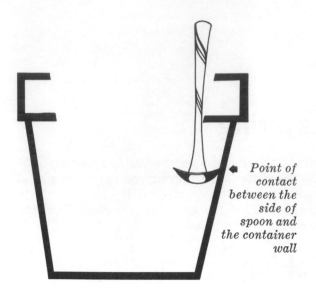

← *Point of contact between the side of spoon and the container wall*

Tilt spoon until sand begins to fall in either a soft mound or sharp peak, as desired.

Mounding

The next technique, mounding, also has many applications. It is critical here to learn how to hold the spoon as mounds of sand are poured.

First establish a point of contact between the spoon's side and the wall of the container. This contact point will serve as a pivot and, more importantly, a means of steadying the spoon as the sand is poured.

Fill the spoon with sand and position its side against the inside container wall over the area where you want the mound to be. Holding the spoon in the same position, gradually tilt the spoon until the sand begins to fall from the spoon's tip. Be sure the spoon is positioned within the container close to where the sand is to fall. Holding the spoon too high or too far away from the container's base will result in a rounded mound. A sharp peak can be achieved by pouring the sand close to the desired position. These mounds can be done individually, to create a landscape with hills and mountains of appropriate colors, or in a series, to make a harlequin pattern of bright colors.

Landscape example depicting layer of ground level with hills and mountains (sky layer in place).

Example of harlequin design (diamond pattern).

III
GEOMETRIC PATTERNS

Two contrasting colors in layers.

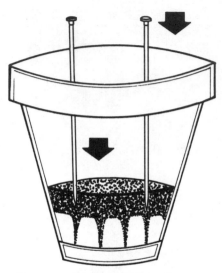

Press needle through base layer.

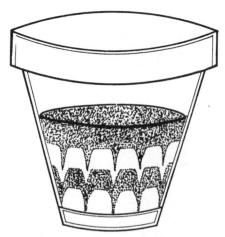

Example of simple layered ribbon design. Layers three and four repeat the pattern of layers one and two. Needle is poked through to top of layer one.

RIBBON DESIGNS

In the preliminary exercises, the fundamentals of geometric patterns were practiced. Now we will cover the basic ribbon patterns.

In the base of the container, begin by spooning two layers of contrasting sand. These may be of equal or different depths.

After this base is completed, use the size five knitting needle to create the design. Hold the needle against the glass and, as was done in the primary exercise, make impressions through the layers to the bottom of the container. You could place more than two layers in the container initially and press through all of them simultaneously.

This design scheme is very simple and easy to do; however, more pleasing results are achieved if you follow the instructions here to create a staggered ribbon design.

Continue by placing a third layer, of contrasting color (or repeat the first color used), over the two poked layers. Use the knitting needle to press through this layer in an alternating pattern between the first impressions, either down to the bottom of the container or only down until the tip of the impression touches the top of the initial layer. Use the illustrations for further clarification.

The design scheme has now been set. Continue adding layers and using the knitting needle to make impressions in an alternating pattern.

Alternating layers and impressions.

For alternating ribbon design, add third layer.

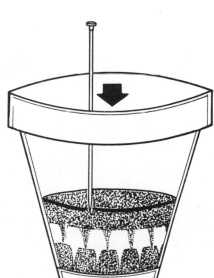

Poke in an alternating fashion between the first impressions down to the top of initial layer.

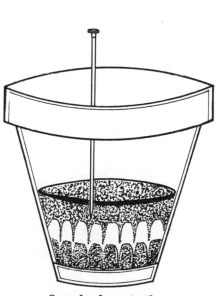

Or poke down to the bottom of the container for a different pattern.

THE STAR RIBBON

For some variation of design, it is quite simple to employ the knitting needle in a different manner, by changing the angle as the needle is inserted in the sand.

For this design pattern, it is necessary to place all of the layers of sand in the container first. Remember to carefully consider the colors you choose. Different shades of green with alternating layers of yellow is an attractive combination. Brown, tan, orange, and yellow—with thin layers of black sand between each layer—provide a subtle but striking base for the greenery that will be added later.

*Press needle through
layers at 45 degree angles.*

*Press through layers
in opposite direction.*

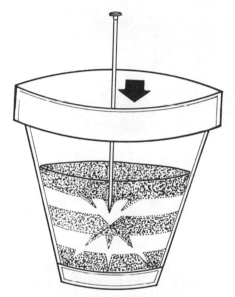

*Press straight down, intersecting
existing impressions.*

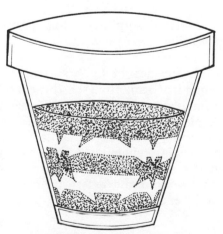

Finished star ribbon design.

After the colored sand layers are in place, begin to make impressions in the sand in the same manner as before, holding the needle against the glass. Press down through the layers holding the needle at approximately a forty-five degree angle for the first impression. Make the next one holding the needle at the same angle, but in the opposite direction. In other words, the second impression should cross the first one, creating an "X" design. You may use an angle other than forty-five degrees if desired. The size of the container will determine how many impressions you can make, but the angle used is governed only by what you think is most attractive. After the initial "X" is made, make another impression straight down between the two angular ones, intersecting the point where the "X" crosses.

When completed, this variation on the ribbon design should look like a simple star pattern all around the container.

Other variations on the basic designs illustrated here can be made by using your imagination and employing other tools to make your impressions. Try using pencils, forks, popsicle sticks, almost anything around the house. All of these suggested tools will make different impressions as they are pressed through the sand layers. Experiment in a water glass before you try new tools.

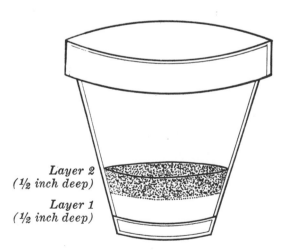

Plant stake

Layer 2
(½ inch deep)

Layer 1
(½ inch deep)

INDIAN BLANKET DESIGN

Take a tip from the American Indians' talent for making geometric designs. There are some very good books available on the subject of crafts and weaving. From these, new design patterns, like the one we will describe here, can be derived.

For this particular design, an ordinary wooden, plant identification stake was used.

Begin to form the design by first placing two layers of sand in the bottom of the container. Make them fairly deep, almost one-half inch each. Holding the plant stake firmly against the glass, press down through the layers until a square impression is made. Remember to pull back from the side of the container and then out. After repeating this around the entire container, use the brush to level off the top layer.

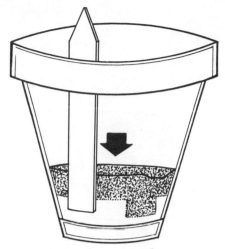

Press down to make a
square impression.

Use brush to smooth top layer.

Add another layer of sand (again fairly deep). You have the option of using either the pointed, V-shaped end of the plant stake or the artist's brush to make the next set of impressions; use whichever is most comfortable. Make a V-shaped impression over each square. The brush will remove the sand from the side of the glass, and as the sand falls away, the V shape will form. Keep brushing until the top of the V is as wide as the top of the square impression. Use the knitting needle if necessary to make the bottom of the V more pointed. Spoon in a layer of your contrasting shade to fill the large V-shaped impressions.

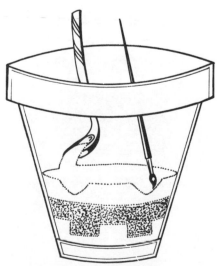

Use brush to form V-shaped
impressions in third layer.

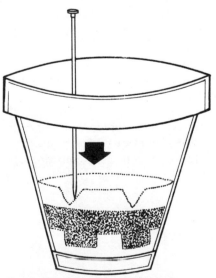

Use knitting needle gently to make
bottom of V more pointed.

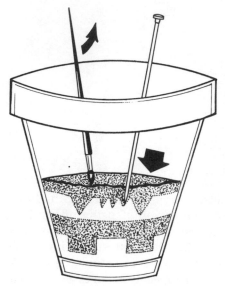

After adding contrasting layer, use brush and knitting needle to make smaller V's.

Level off top layer.

Use the brush and knitting needle to make smaller *V* impressions between the larger ones. You should have enough room between the large *V*'s for two of these. Again use the brush to level off this layer, as it will become uneven as you work. (Add some sand if necessary to achieve a level surface.)

When this is completed, you may repeat the entire pattern or stop where you are, depending on the amount of room the container provides.

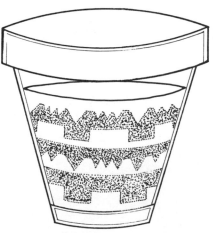

Finished Indian blanket design.

*Add more sand.
The firebird will be formed
within this layer.*

FIREBIRD DESIGN

As an addition to the Indian blanket design, add a firebird in a bright color for variation and interest. After the initial layers with square indentations are in place, add more sand to the top layer instead of leveling it off. Brush away a V-shaped indentation and smooth the sand on either side of the V, creating a slight incline as you brush; the steepest part should be about one and one-half inches from each side of the V. Fill the V and the brushed-out section with a brightly colored sand.

*Brush away a V shape. Create
an incline at each side as shown.*

Fill brushed-out area.

Use the knitting needle to poke on each side of the *V* as indicated by the illustration. These impressions will form the fanned-out tail of the bird. Level off the mound of sand covering the inclined area so that the wing surfaces will be smooth. Spoon a mound over the tail area for the bird's neck. Cover the wings with the background color, leaving the top of the neck exposed.

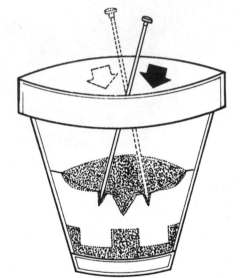

Poke for fanned tail.

Brush to smooth wing surfaces.

Pour mound for neck.

Cover, leaving top of neck mound exposed.

Add a small mound of sand over the neck and extend it to one side. If you need clarification, check the illustration. This small mound will be the bird's head. Now cover all of this with the background sand. Continue and finish the design by making more square-shaped impressions over the firebird. Check the previous lesson if you have any problem.

Pour small mound for head on one side of the neck.

Cover all and finish the pattern by repeating the blanket design.

IV
SEASCAPES

THE BASIC OCEAN

Color blending is the critical part of creating an ocean with color alone. Start by choosing appropriate colors. Blend various shades of blue and green together in a cup. The secret to arriving at a streaky look to the ocean is to mix the colors together only slightly. Add all of the colors to the cup. Then, mix with the spoon, bringing the spoon up through all the colors only two or three times. Add some white sand last, being careful not to mix it in too thoroughly, so that a "salt and pepper" look is avoided. If you are clever with the color blending, the effects are terrific. As you spoon in the ocean and gradually fill the container, add more dark blue to the mixture. This will, by small degrees, change the color of the water to a darker shade as the horizon line is reached. The ocean always looks darker on the horizon line. For good examples of this effect, try looking through travel brochures.

Blended ocean.

CRASHING WAVES

An ocean can also be depicted by building individual, white-capped waves in a series. The illusion of action is easily rendered and best used in the foreground of an oceanscape, gradually changing to a blended ocean for the background waters. The technique used to form the white-caps will serve as a valuable tool to be applied in future lessons. Begin by mounding a teaspoon of sea-colored sand against the wall of the container. Top this mound with approximately three-quarters of a teaspoon of white sand. It is very important that the white sand is applied correctly. When the tip of the spoon is in position over the sea-colored mound (it should be touching the top of the sea-mound), tilt the spoon, making a slight indentation in the top of the mound. This indentation will enable you to concentrate the bulk of the white sand in the crest of the wave, with only small amounts falling down the slopes of the mound. After some practice, making the indentation and pouring the

Pour mound of sea color.

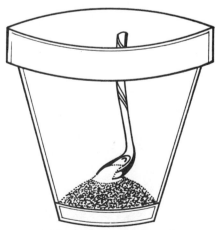

Add white cap. Spoon tip contacts mound to make indentation as white sand is poured.

Upholstery needle in position with motion indicated.

Jab quickly, dragging the needle sideways.

Example of crashing waves combined with ocean technique.

white sand will become a smooth, single motion. A curling, breaking wave usually has more foam on the crest, exactly what we are rendering here.

Use the sharpest instrument available—the upholstery needle is best—to jab the white into the sea-colored sand. Be sure to hold the needle tightly against the glass and, with a slight dragging motion, jab quickly along the entire mound. The sideways motion in combination with clever jabbing will blur the white to suggest the frothy crest of the wave.

Make each wave individually until the entire container base is covered. As was mentioned earlier, you may want to combine the blended ocean method with breaking waves to achieve a more realistic scene. Perspective plays a very important part in any good quality sand painting. To best translate the illusion of distance in sand, make the initial layer of breakers rather large, graduating to smaller ones as you continue to build crashing waves. When the white-capped waves have taken about half of the area of the container designated for the ocean, begin to layer blended blues and greens over the breakers. Remember to intersperse some white sand into the mixture and to add darker colors of blue as you progress. The final result should be a dark-blue horizon line coming down to lighter blues and greens, with the breaking waves in the foreground.

SHORELINES

Shoreline around entire container.

Now that the foundation for a good ocean-scape has been learned, the formation of land masses that will complete the ocean vista is next on the agenda.

A shoreline is easily formed by spooning a layer of either beige or tan sand directly over the ocean's surface at the horizon line. If you so choose, extend this layer around the entire container. If, however, you want to portray the existence of a tropical island, make the beach area or shoreline encompass only part of the container, perhaps three to four inches in length, depending on the circumference of the container. Taper this layer on the ends so that the beach will gradually slope into the ocean.

On this island, or shorebase, build foothills and mountains by employing the basic mounding techniques learned in the initial instructions. Choose your colors carefully so there will be good contrast between the foothills and the shore. Remember as you are constructing these hills that perspective is very important. Land masses appear darker as distance increases. Nature can be duplicated with the clever use of colors. Make your first layer of foothills tan, the next dark brown, and finally the largest mounds, mountains, of black sand.

First fill your spoon with the lightest shade of tan and pour a series of foothills. Continue as indicated in the illustration to pour additional mounds. Remember to place the spoon's side against the container wall and gradually tilt the spoon until the sand flows into a mound.

Island tapering into the sea.

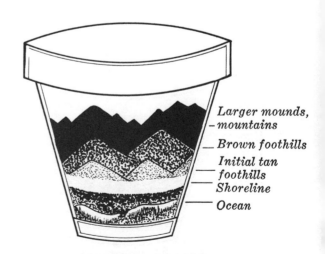

Larger mounds, mountains
Brown foothills
Initial tan foothills
Shoreline
Ocean

NOTE: In order to stabilize the mountains, it will be necessary to cover them with a sky mixture. You may, of course, use a solid-color sky; a blend, however, has more eye appeal. In an empty cup, mix (blend colors together only slightly) some light-blue sand with white; or, if a sunset sky is desired, blend yellow and orange sand together.

Spoon the sky mixture in between each mountain first; then gradually build the sky level until the mountains are covered. If there are any difficulties, check back to the preliminary exercises for more information. If you have mixed the colors correctly, the sky should be streaky and natural.

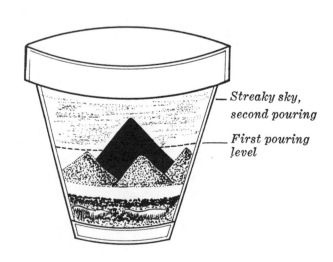

Streaky sky, second pouring

First pouring level

VOLCANOES

Capping dark mountain (volcano) with red sand.

Jabbing red.

For a really different and interesting tropical isle motif, build a volcano on your island!

After you have completed some foothills and mountains, you can begin the volcano by first mixing some black, dark blue, and perhaps a small amount of purple or gray sand together for the base. Pour a mound in the normal fashion. Now, pause and think back to the ocean waves with their white crests. Cap the top of the volcano in the same manner as the wave—topping it with red sand instead of white. Remember to make a small dip in the top of the mound as you position the red sand on top, letting it run down the slopes of the volcano as was done for the ocean wave.

After the red sand has been applied, use the upholstery needle to jab the red sand into the mound.

*Add additional sand
to peak, if necessary.*

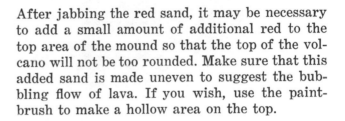

*Brush out hollow
within peak area.*

After jabbing the red sand, it may be necessary to add a small amount of additional red to the top area of the mound so that the top of the volcano will not be too rounded. Make sure that this added sand is made uneven to suggest the bubbling flow of lava. If you wish, use the paintbrush to make a hollow area on the top.

When the volcano is complete, cover it with sky, supporting the slopes first, then covering the top. An added point of interest might be some gray sand layered over the top of the volcano, interspersed with the sky mixture, to suggest smoke from the burning lava.

*OPTIONAL: Smoke coming
from volcano top.*

BREAKING SURF

Begin by first completing a fairly calm ocean in the base of the container. Intersperse some white sand as you add the water colors you have already blended. Jab the white streaks as you progress, especially as you get to the horizon line. You may also position some breaking waves near the area where the island will be. Position the island next, tapering it into the sea, and define it with a thin layer of black. Be sure to make this black layer fairly thin, as you will next be adding rocks.

Mix some black and gray sand for the rocks. Remember not to stir the colors too well so that there will be some color variation as the mounds are poured.

Thin covering of black for detail. Gray and black rock mixture.

Construct your rocky shoreline by first pouring mounds of the gray-black mixture on the beach area. Outline each mound with a thin covering of black to differentiate between one rock and another if you think that this is needed. Use your own judgment.

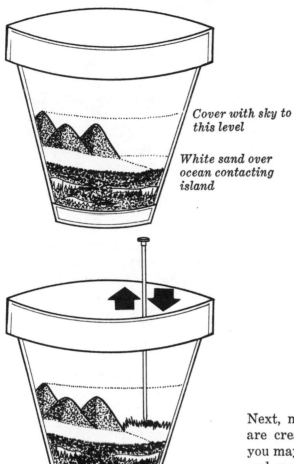

Cover with sky to
this level

White sand over
ocean contacting
island

Jab into white for
crashing surf.

Pull white up and
blur for spray effect.

Next, mix some sky colors. Since the scene we
are creating could suggest a stormy condition,
you may want to use a blend of light blue, white,
and gray. The crashing waves we will construct
could suggest a time of day when the tide is coming in. In this case, it would be apropos to mix
a sunset sky (orange, yellow, and pink). After
you have decided on the color scheme, spoon
some white sand over the water's surface near
the island. Then cover the water area and the
white layer with the sky mixture to the level of
the rock mounds already in place.

Now we are ready to create the crashing surf
against the rocky shore. With the needle against
the glass, jab into the white surf area. Use the
needle to blur the white with an upward stroke
as indicated by the arrows in the illustration.
Place the needle into the white sand and as you
move the needle's tip upward, pull some of the
white sand up and slightly over the rocks. This
will create a spray effect if you are careful to
position the blurred white sand in contact with
or very close to the rock mounds.

Pour more rock mounds.

Cover with sky.

If you think you need more rocks, pour a few extra mounds of the gray-black mixture on top of the original ones. Take care so as not to overlap any gray on the sky already in place. Correct any overlap that may occur with the artist's brush. Now cover the entire rock area with more sky so that you can add shape to the rocks with the needle.

Place the needle firmly against the glass and through the sand. Locate the tip of the needle in the vicinity of the rock mounds. Gently and slowly, push against the sky-colored sand only. By pushing on the sky-colored sand in proximity to the rocks, you will gradually move the gray sand. If you carefully watch what you are doing and push from several different angles, the rocks can be made to appear jagged and more angular in shape as opposed to the smooth mounds originally poured.

This technique of pushing against a background color to force another color or form into shape will be valuable to you in future lessons.

Locate needle in sky near rocks.

Push against the sky sand. Rock mounds will move from pressure of sky color against gray, producing jagged effect.

LIGHTHOUSES

A rocky island motif could be further enhanced by adding a lighthouse. Here, the shaping technique just learned will be instrumental.

On an existing island scene, begin by mounding some white sand onto the island base. Make this mound fairly large and concentrated in a specific area. In other words, pour a tall, peaked mound instead of an easy, rounded one. Choose a sky mixture and surround the white mound with these colors.

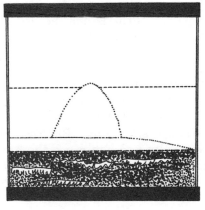

Sky mixture to this level

White mound

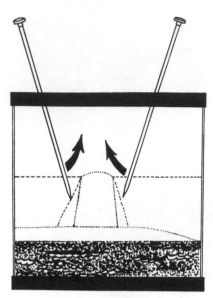

*Dotted lines indicate
original mound.*

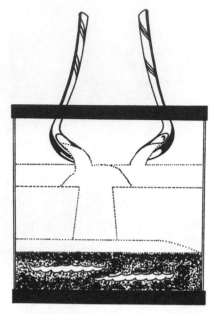

*Pour second mound of white.
Support with sky.*

Place the needle as before against the glass through the sky. Use an upward sweeping stroke to make the white mound's sides upright. An exact vertical form is not needed. Most lighthouses are wider at the bottom and taper as they go higher.

Add height to the lighthouse by spooning another mound of white over the white base already formed so that the new mound rises above the existing sky level. Buttress this mound with more sky and again use the needle to form this mound into the upright sides of the lighthouse. Brush away any sky that may have fallen over the white while shaping.

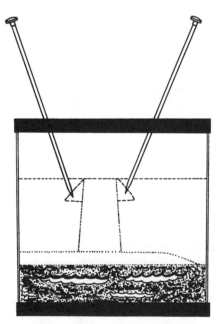

*Make sides upright. Dotted
lines indicate initial mound.*

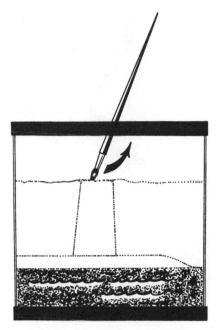

Brush away top for neatness.
Add thin layer of yellow
on sky at one side.

On one side of the lighthouse, on the sky level that is still exposed, layer some yellow. You may use the needle to blur the yellow out and away from the lighthouse. Alternate some thin sky layers with the yellow sand. These will form the lighthouse beams. Add a small mound of white over the lighthouse structure and surround with sky; then shape the white with the needle to complete the lighthouse tower.

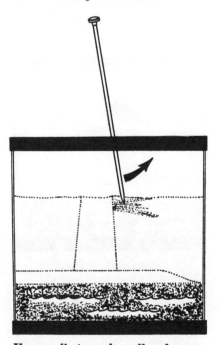

Use needle to make yellow beams.

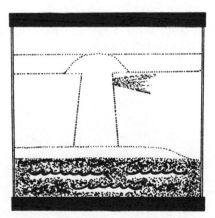

Pour more white and surround with sky.

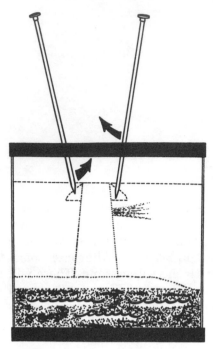

*Shape top section as before and
level with brush.*

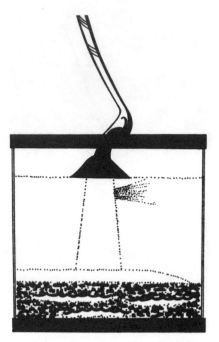

Pour peaked mound for roof.

Level the sky and tower-top area with the brush.
Cap the tower with a triangular peaked mound
of black or red. Now that the roof is in place,
cover everything with sky.

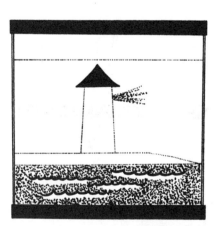

Finished lighthouse.

ADVANCED LIGHTHOUSES

Since this is the first experience you have had thus far with advanced shaping techniques, do not become discouraged if your first lighthouse is not perfectly symmetrical. Remember good sand sculpture takes practice! When you have become more skilled in making forms with upright sides, you can improve upon this basic lighthouse by making the tower in two colors. Simply alternate colors as you construct the tower one layer at a time. Another change in detail is to make a wider top on the tapered tower. The illustrations should be sufficient instruction since the techniques needed have already been explained.

Finished advanced lighthouse.

This lighthouse takes more time to construct, but the principles are the same. The essential thing is to take your time and plan each step before you proceed. Using the needle to form the upright sides is the most important technique here. Practice first if you need confidence.

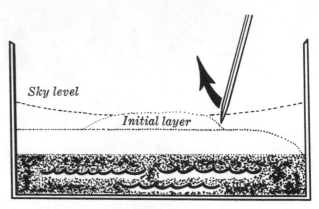

CLOSE-UP VIEW

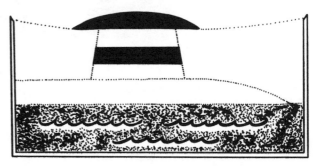

CLOSE-UP VIEW
Build tower one layer at a time, alternating colors as you go. Add supporting sky as necessary.
EXAMPLE:
1. layer white mound for base, add sky and shape.
2. layer black, add sky and shape, etc.

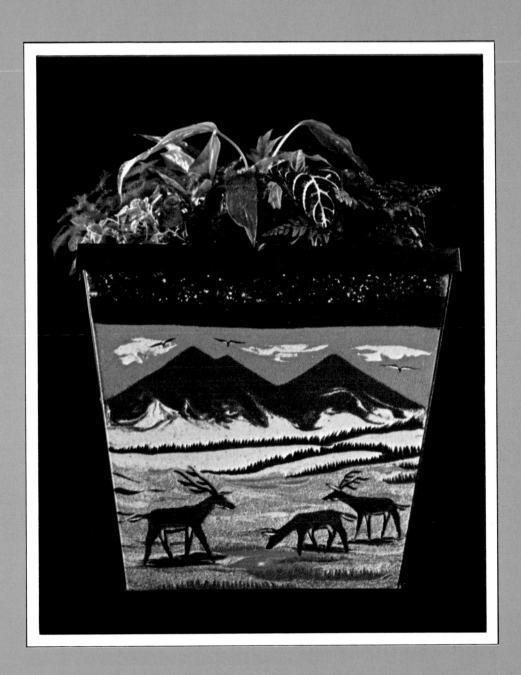

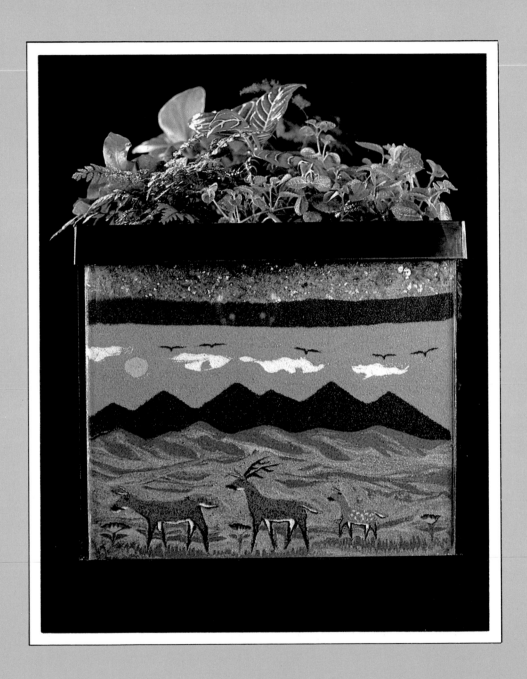

WHALES

Sea creatures are interesting and simple to do. A whale is very easy to make and is a sure topic of conversation. Begin by first making an ocean in the base of the container. You can combine this idea with the island pattern you have already learned. Make the whale on one side, the island on the opposite side for an "in the round" effect.

After the water is completed, layer a bit of gray or black over the ocean surface to form the base of the whale's body. On the left side (the whale's head), spoon a thin layer of black (if you are making a black body make a gray layer here). Make this thin line about an eighth of the entire length of the initial layer. This will be the whale's mouth.

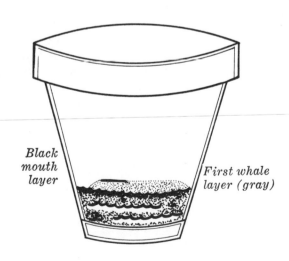

Black mouth layer

First whale layer (gray)

*Pour two mounds over initial base.
The mouth becomes evident.*

Now make a large mound of the body color
(gray), covering the mouth and three-quarters
of the whale's length. Over the remaining length
of the body, pour a small mound, connecting it
to the larger mound.

Decide on some sky colors; after you have mixed
them, set them aside for a few minutes while
you shape the mounds with your artist's brush.
Run the brush over the area where the smaller
mound meets the larger one so that you create
a gentle valley shape. You may also want to
round off the larger mound if it is too peaked.

*Use brush to smooth the
whale's profile.*

Apply the sky color over all until you have at
least one-half inch of sky depth over the highest
part of the shape. Use the number five knitting
needle at a forty-five degree angle to poke into
the side of the smaller mound (at the end) to
make two fins of the whale's tail. The sky will
fall into place, dividing the tail fin. Use the
needle again to push the bottom tail fin, a little
at a time, closer to the water line. Hold the
needle against the glass to push it into position
as necessary.

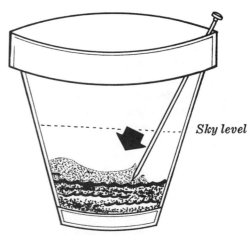

Sky level

*Poke into end of mound
for tail fins.*

Needle used to divide tail fins and to push bottom fin down closer to the water line. Push gradually.

Pour mound of white.

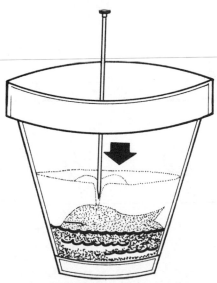

Use needle to poke down white.

Remember it is better to go slowly and gradually when you shape the tail fins. Do not expect to do this with one stroke. Withdraw the needle carefully after each poke so that you can more accurately judge the amount of correction still needed.

Now you can add a water spout. Place a mound of white over the whale's head. Use a thin, pointed needle to poke the white down through the sky until it is *almost* touching the whale's body. (Do not poke down too far or you will damage the smooth mound you have created.) You will probably have to poke more than one time to get enough white down through the sky so it will look like a water spout. Leave the extra white from the mound you poured. (Be sure it is not too much.) This excess will appear to be the wide spray at the top of the water spout. You can now correct the whale's nose if it needs rounding by holding the needle against the glass and pushing gently on the sky color. Now, cover everything with sky.

*Shape nose so that it is more
rounded. (Dotted line indicates
original nose position.)*

The finished whale should have a divided tail fin,
a water spout with extra white on top for spray,
a black mouth, and a rounded, almost blunt nose.

If you want more detail, add an eye. After placing the whale's mouth, pour only part of the
large mound. Place just a dab of black sand in
a small notch made with the artist's brush. Then
finish making the large mound. The dab of black
will be sufficient for the whale's eye.

Finished whale with water spout.

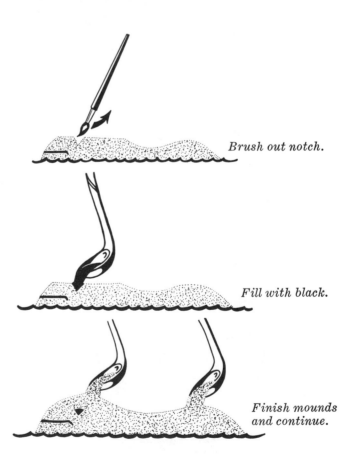

Brush out notch.

Fill with black.

*Finish mounds
and continue.*

UNDERWATER SCENES: FISH

Build a sandy bottom in the base of the container and add some rock-type mounds, in varying shapes of brown. Pour a few deep, short layers of dark green here and there around the container.

Mix a few sea-colored shades together and cover the rock areas and green layers with about one inch of sand. Use the needle against the glass to push on the sea color, thus moving the rocks into more jagged forms. To add further interest, jab the needle (again against the glass) down into the dark green layers already in place for sea vegetation. The same technique was used with the ocean wave and the volcano top.

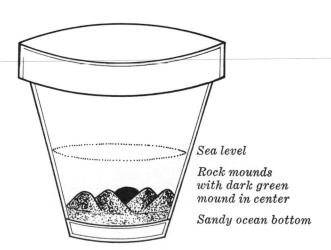

Sea level

*Rock mounds
with dark green
mound in center*

Sandy ocean bottom

*Use needle to push
rocks into more irregular shapes.
(Push against sea color.)*

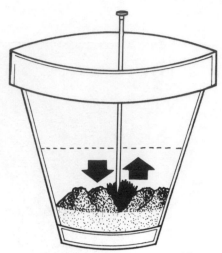

Jab dark green for sea vegetation.

After the ocean floor has been completed, use the artist's brush to remove a semicircular area approximately the size of the fish you plan to make. Choose a color for the fish's body; we will use orange in this lesson. Fill the indentation with orange to the level of the water.

*Use brush to remove sea color
in round shape.*

Fill brushed-out area with orange.

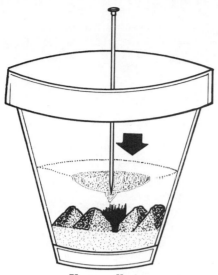

*Use needle to
poke down, creating belly fin.*

*Sea color overlaps body at left
side to form mouth. Spoon orange on
right side for bottom tail fin.*

Use your knitting needle to poke down through the fish's belly area to create a bottom fin. To make the mouth, spoon a bit of the sea color so that it overlaps the fish's form on the left side. At the right side (over the exposed water level), pour a bit of orange for the bottom tail fin.

On the right side, where the bottom tail fin was just poured, cover the orange with a sloping layer of the sea color.

Cover orange at right side with sea color.

Cover with more orange over sea color. Mound should be large, to cover sea on left, creating the mouth, and to create top tail fin.

Next spoon a rather large mound as indicated by the illustration for the rest of the fish's body. Use the artist's brush to trim away some of the mound over the tail area, as the fish's body should taper some near the tail. This large mound, when poured, completes the open mouth of the fish and the top tail fin. Cover the fish's body with sea color to stabilize it but leave the very crest of the body still exposed.

Trim tail section with brush.

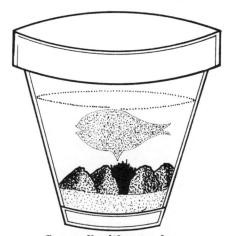

Cover all with sea color, leaving top of body exposed.

Pour orange mound for top fin.

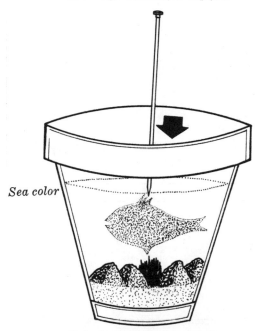

Sea color

Poke top tail fin for detail.

On the exposed crest of the fish's back, spoon a small amount of sand in a mound for a back fin. Cover this new mound with sea color and jab into it slightly for detail.

If you want to add more detail, add an eye to the fish in the same manner used for the addition of the whale's eye. Brush away a notch and add a bit of black before you complete the fish's body.

Finished fish with optional eye.

SAILBOATS

A sailboat is a graceful vessel and an enhancing addition to an ocean motif.

Spoon in an ocean base on which to build your vessel. With the artist's brush, make a hollow on the ocean's surface. Make the hollow taper in the front (or on the left side) in an easy slope. The back—or right side—should be more vertical to provide for the stern of the boat. Do not concern yourself with creating perfect hollows; corrections can be made later. Most of the attention will probably focus on the billowing sail. When the hollow has been formed, fill it to the water line with black or brown and use the brush to level the surface (deck area).

Brush out hollow for hull.

Fill in hollow with black, and level.

*Cover hull with
thin layer of sky so that the sea is
covered on each end.*

Choose some sky colors for the background as you will need to stabilize the sail before any shaping can take place. Over the hull, which should now be level, spoon a very thin layer of the sky mixture. Extend the layer over the ocean surface at each end of the hull at least one-half to one inch. Be sure that it is level.

On this base of sky, spoon in a large, peaked mound of white sand for the sail over the hull. Make the sail any color you wish—we will refer to white here. After the large mound is in place, cover it with the previously prepared sky mixture. Surround the sides of the sail first, then gradually cover the peak until a depth of at least one-half inch is obtained.

With the upholstery needle, if one is available, or a size one knitting needle (the thinnest instrument available), poke down through the center of the mound, peak to bottom. The sky will be pushed down the center of the sail, dividing the mound into two halves. It will probably be necessary to repeat this stroke more than once to achieve good separation.

Pour large white mound on sky for sail.

Cover with sky in stages as indicated.

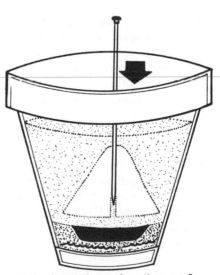

*Poke down through sail mound.
This may have to be repeated.*

NOTE: When the sail is divided, expect the mound to collapse and become misshapen. If there is not enough sky over the peak, this will be evident, as the white sail mound will become exposed. If you see this happening as you poke, add more sky over the peak area before proceeding with a second stroke.

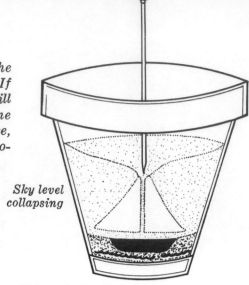

Sky level collapsing

This an indication that more sky is needed. Correct this before the second dividing stroke is initiated.

Be sure that as you do this the exact path of the needle is followed each time. When the sail has been divided, use the thin needle again to shape the sail into final position. Remember to remove the needle by leaning it back and towards the center of the container after each poke. As you learned with the lighthouse sides, place the needle in the sky-colored sand and locate its tip in the vicinity of the sail by firmly placing the tip against the glass. Begin near the bottom of the mound and use a firm, upward, angular stroke to push against the sky color. This will in turn shape the side of the sail into a smooth, even slope. Do each side separately.

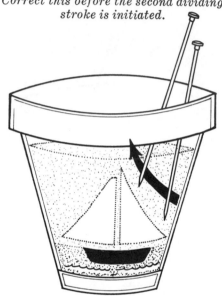

Shape sail with the needle against the glass. Use an angular, upward stroke.

With any shaping exercise, the weight of the background sand is important in that it provides stability, making the shaping possible. If there is any difficulty encountered, it is a good "rule of thumb" to add additional support behind, around, or over the form being shaped, as the case may be.

A bright, small yacht flag may be placed over the sail. After the sail has been shaped with the needle, brush away a notch. (Same procedure as for the whale and fish eyes.) Within the notch, spoon a small amount of red, blue, or any bright-colored sand. Cover the addition with sky and use the needle to shape the flag as necessary.

Shape other side in the same manner.

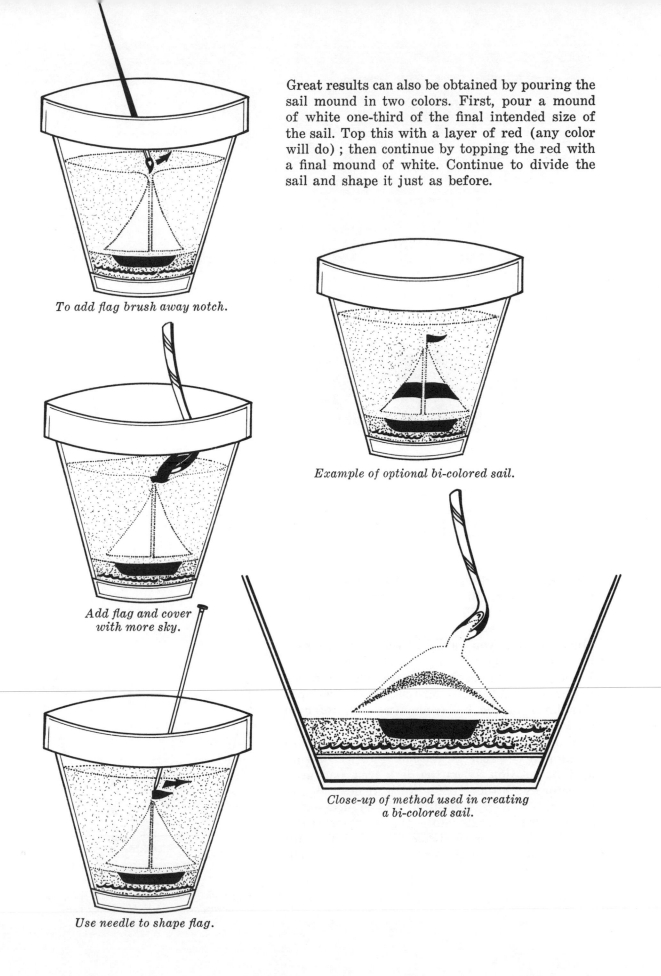

Great results can also be obtained by pouring the sail mound in two colors. First, pour a mound of white one-third of the final intended size of the sail. Top this with a layer of red (any color will do); then continue by topping the red with a final mound of white. Continue to divide the sail and shape it just as before.

To add flag brush away notch.

Example of optional bi-colored sail.

Add flag and cover with more sky.

Use needle to shape flag.

Close-up of method used in creating a bi-colored sail.

CLIPPER SHIPS

The interesting thing about clipper ships is their array of sails. But these vessels are easily formed, as you shall see.

Much of what you have learned about the sailboat can be applied here. Build an ocean base. When you brush out the hull area, make it larger than before. When you fill the hollow, overlap a thin layer of the hull color (we will refer to brown here) on the ocean level at the front (bow) of the ship. Use the needle against the glass to straighten the rear of the hull (stern) into an upright position. Level the deck area (surface) as before with the artist's brush. If desired, you can leave the rear position of the deck at a slight upward angle, since clipper ships traditionally have massive sterns. Cover with a thin layer of sky extending over each end of the hull.

Brush away hull.

Fill hollow, overlapping hull color on ocean surface in the bow area.

Use needle to form stern into a more vertical position.

Level off deck. The stern can be left at a higher level if desired.

Next, spoon a large (fairly thick) layer (not mounded) of white sand over the sky layer. Be sure that this white layer extends over each end of the hull, at least up to the front end of the hull extension, the prow. Level this layer (pour number one) off so that it is uniform. Cover the white layer with another thin layer of sky; build up the sky at the sides of this white layer so that a level sky is achieved (pour number two).

Cover the hull with a thin layer of sky.

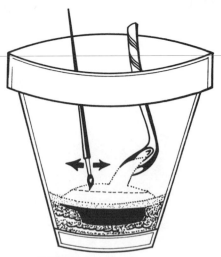

POUR 1:
Spoon in white and level.

POUR 2:
Cover white with sky and level.

POUR 3:
Spoon more white on and level.

Add another layer of white, a bit shorter in length this time, over the thin, separating sky and level it (pour number three). Cover with sky again, building the areas to the immediate right and left of the white layer as you go and leaving another level sky layer behind (pour number four). Now, add the third and final white top sail. This addition should be a mound rather than a flat thick layer (pour number five).

Cover all. Study the drawings and the progression exhibited. (Place one-half to one inch of sky over sail peak.)

POUR 4:
Cover with sky as before. Level.

POUR 5:
Spoon in final mound of white.

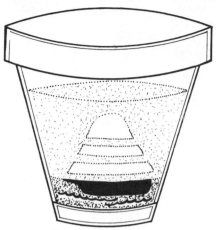

Cover top of mound with at least one-half inch of sky. Finished rough sail structure.

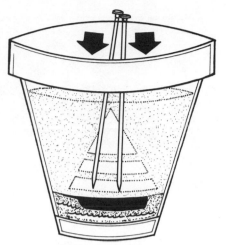

Poke at opposing angles to divide the sail.

With the size one knitting needle, poke through all of the sail layers at the two angles shown. Add sky if necessary and poke through the layers enough to create a clear division. These sails usually do not need more than one poke. Next, reshape the sides or edges of the sails collectively as you did in the sailboat lesson.

By now you should be getting the "feel of the sand." When you shape the sand with the needle against the glass, begin to rely on your own judgment with respect to necessary corrections or adjustments. Your imagination should also be one of your greatest aids. Experiment! Often, improved and different techniques are quite accidentally discovered.

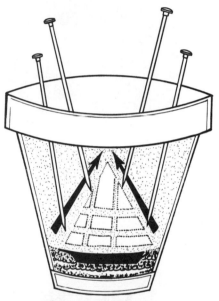

Shape sail edges. Use needle against the glass technique.

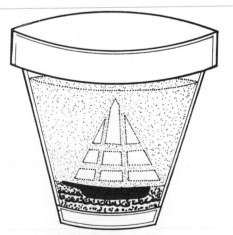

Finished clipper ship.

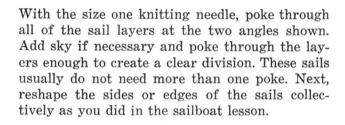

Pour mound on deck.

FISHING BOATS

Begin this vessel in the usual manner on a pre-made ocean base. Clear out the hull area and fill it with any desired color. On the deck surface, after it has been leveled with the brush, spoon a mound of white. Be sure that the mound is not too large. Level it with the brush just as the lower sail of the clipper ship was done. To make a cabin window on this white surface brush out a notch (try to make the bottom of it fairly level) and fill it with a small amount of black sand.

Level off.

Brush out notch.

Fill in notch with black.

Cover the filled notch with white—the amount will depend on how tall you want the cabin to be. With the needle tip against the glass, push on the sides of the black and gradually force it into a rectangular shape. Make the sides upright; then run the needle tip across the top of the black until it is level.

Cover notch and shape window.

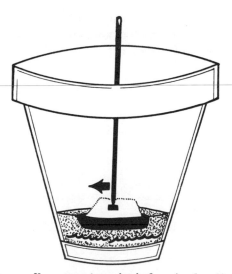

Run needle across top of window for leveling.

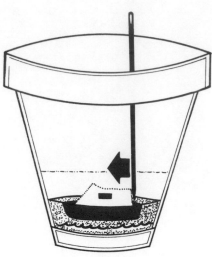

Cover with sky.
Position upright sides of cabin.

Smooth cabin roof.

Finished fishing boat.

While the window was being shaped, the cabin area surely became misshapen. Cover the entire vessel with a prepared sky mixture. Shape the cabin sides and top, holding the needle firmly against the glass and pushing against the sky sand.

This simple boat can be used in many different scenes to depict various types of boats by simply changing the colors used for the hull and cabin. For example, make the hull white and add some extra windows in the cabin to create a cabin cruiser. Let the background you create govern the type of vessel that you make.

Example of yacht or cruiser.

SUNSET, WINTER, AND STORMY SKIES

Streaky sky accomplished by mixing colors.

Since you have been mixing simple blended skies in previous chapters, we will devote some time here to mixing techniques and color coordination.

The traditional blue sky can be further enhanced with the addition of small amounts of white, lavender, or yellow. The best aid you have for new color combinations is close at hand. Study nature in photographs and by becoming aware of what is around you. Inspiration will come easily after viewing a few evening sunsets.

Use an empty container to mix your skies. Add all of the shades you plan to employ at once; then use your spoon to mix them carefully. Bring the spoon up through the colors only three or four times. By following these instructions, the colors will be only partially mixed. When the mixture is spooned into the container a multi-layered look will result. The spoon should hold several colors each time it is dipped into the mixing container.

It would be a good idea to try out new color combinations in a drinking glass first. Sometimes combinations that do not seem too appealing are quite attractive when you see them together.

Here the key is clever color mixing. Use subdued shades with white interspersed to suggest falling snow or rain. These subtle skies are quite effective when you combine them with snow-capped mountains and landscapes that depend on stark, dark, tree lines and woodland for impact. The composition of the sky should always complement the land or seascape.

Finished cumulus cloud.

72

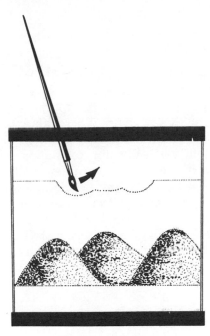

Brush out hollows.

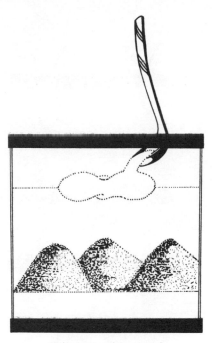

*Fill with white sand,
mounding the white as you pour.*

Clouds are a very important addition to any sky for interest. Since they are rather abstract in nature they are not difficult to render in sand. What you have already learned "technique-wise" will serve you well here. Cumulus clouds are the fluffy, cotton-ball type. Begin these by first distorting the sky surface with the brush. Make several rounded impressions. Mound in some white sand to fill the hollows and provide mounds of white over the existing sky level.

Now cover the white sand with the premixed sky. The billowiness of this cloud type is achieved by using the needle against the glass. As you have done in the past, insert the needle through the sky in the vicinity of the cloud to form and shape the cloud into rounded, roly-poly lobes. Round off the sides and top. Your control over the needle in this shaping technique will prepare you for other, more difficult assignments and give you an opportunity to practice and increase your skill. Since the cloud, as was mentioned before, is abstract in nature, any imperfections are not a problem. Learn from this exercise.

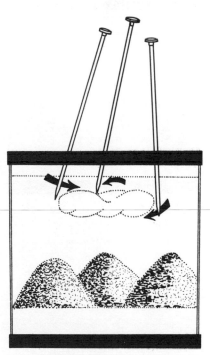

*Shape cloud with
the needle against the glass.*

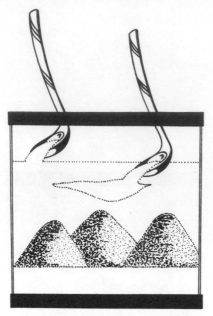

Layer-in white sand and cover.

The second cloud type we will learn about is the wispy, feathery stratus. Simply layer in some white sand as you build up the sky. Cover the white with sky color. When this is done, use the needle to blur the white. Position the needle in the sand vertically approximately one-eighth of an inch from the container wall, *behind* the white sand. Move the needle sideways (holding it upright) behind the white area. The natural shifting of the sand will form a soft, wispy cloud. You may have to repeat this motion several times to achieve the desired amount of feathering.

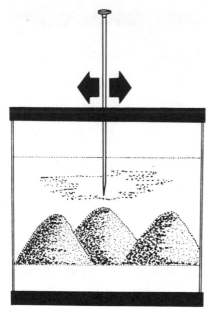

Hold needle vertically. Move in a sideways motion to feather cloud.

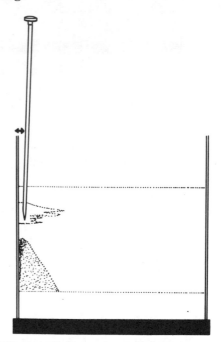

SIDE VIEW: Hold needle behind white area 1/8 inch from side of container.

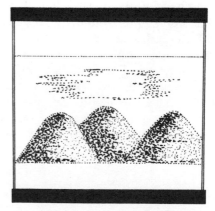

Finished stratus cloud.

RAINBOWS

Within any daytime scene incorporate a colorful rainbow in the design. First, build a basic seascape or landscape. (Land forms will be discussed fully in the next chapters.)

Using a basic landscape with mountains and foothills in place, place a small mound of sky between two mountains; do not build this mound up as high as the peaks of the mountains. It would be helpful for you to find a color spectrum chart, which will give you an idea of the order in which the rainbow colors should be layered across the sky mound.

Place a mound of sky between two mountains.

The first color is usually dark blue, then purple, red, orange, yellow, and light green in that order. Simply layer these colors across the sky mound in an easy arch.

It is not necessary to include all the colors mentioned. Use as many or as few as you wish. If desired, jab through the layers to blend them and then correct the top layer, as it will become uneven from jabbing. If you choose to use this method, be careful not to jab into the underlying sky mound. When you are satisfied with the appearance of the rainbow, cover all with sky.

Mound colors across sky mound.

Jab through colors if desired.

SETTING SUNS

The sun as it sinks below the horizon can be the focal point of many beautiful sand renditions. Color blending in the sky area directly adjacent to the sun is very important, so remember to layer in some bright colors after the sun has been positioned and shaped.

Build a base of light green, with foothills of tan and large mountains. Again, please remember that we will be learning more about landscapes and that you will be able to correlate the setting sun over many more interesting scenes than the simple base you have created here.

Simple landscape base with large mountains.

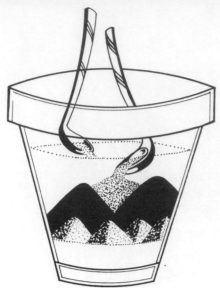

Fill in valley with red and cover with sky.

Use needle to shape sides of red. Place the tip in the area between the mountain's side and the red. Move gradually.

Mix some sky colors together and set them aside. In the valley between two large mountains, spoon a mound of red sand. Its crest should be as high as the mountains' peaks, but should not be so large that any red sand would begin to run down the outer sides of the mountains. (Fill the valley with red sand. This amount should be sufficient.) Cover this mound with the premixed sky, remembering the "center to edge" motion of the spoon. Make the sky at least one-half inch deep over the highest point of the red mound.

Using the needle against the glass, locate it first in the vicinity of the red mound. Push the needle's tip against the sky where the red and the mountain meet. Gradually push the red in away from the mountain and into a rounded shape. Do this on both sides of the red. Take care not to disturb the mountain peaks. Be sure that both sides are round.

After shaping, the sun may develop a pointed top. Use the needle against the glass to correct this or, if you wish, use your spoon to gently pack the sky down, which will push the red into shape.

Method 1: Correct peak with needle.

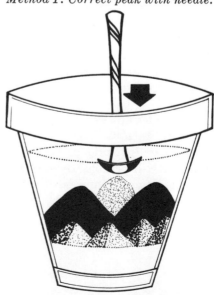

Method 2: Tap on sky surface to push red into shape.

ROUND SUNS

Now that the fundamentals of rounding an existing mound have been learned, you should be ready to take on a more difficult project, forming a round sun. As you will see, the finished form is a very striking addition to the sky. Actually, it looks more difficult than it really is. The natural flow of the sand does much of the work for you.

Form a simple base. Use an ocean, with an island. All you really need is a base upon which you have spooned about half as much sky as you eventually plan to have in the container. On a level area of sky, use your spoon and tap down several times to make a rounded indentation. If you wish, you may use the artist's brush if this seems easier.

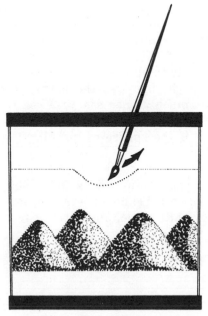

Tap with spoon to create rounded indentation.

Optional method: Use brush to make indentation.

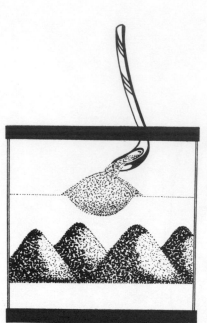

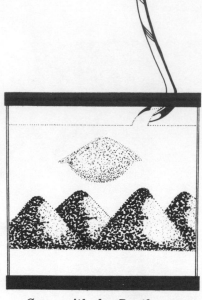

Fill indentation with red, mounding it.

Cover with sky. Depth over peak of red should be ½ inch deep.

Use the needle against the glass to shape the sun.

Spoon red into the hollow until it is completely filled; mound the red into a peak over the indentation. Cover this rough form with at least one-half inch of sky.

Use the needle against the glass to shape the sun. Push against the sky sand to gradually move the sides of the sun. After some practice, you will be able to accomplish this with two strokes, one on each side. Use the needle to correct the sides as much as necessary. When the sides are in position, correct the peak that will form on the top of the sphere by packing the sky down as before.

You may use many colors for either the setting or round sun. Yellow or a mixture of yellow and orange, white alone, pink—try some of your own combinations.

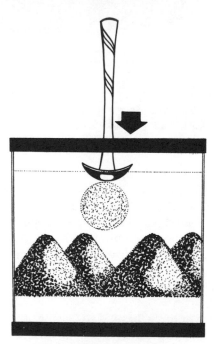

Tap with spoon to remove peak on top of sun.

MOONS AND NIGHT SKIES

Form full moons in a night sky by using the instructions for a round sun. For the sky base, mix dark blue and perhaps a bit of purple.

The crescent moon takes a bit of maneuvering, however. Create a black silhouette of land and mountains. Mix dark blue and purple together for the basic night-sky mixture. (At the end of the lesson, we will go over the construction of a city skyline for an additional application of the moon and night sky.) Over the landscape silhouette, spoon the sky mixture. In the sky, brush out a few notches here and there. In these, spoon a bit of yellow or white. Cover these small mounds with more sky to give the impression of stars. Do not make the stars too large.

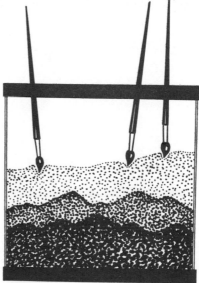

Brush out notches.

Fill notches and cover.

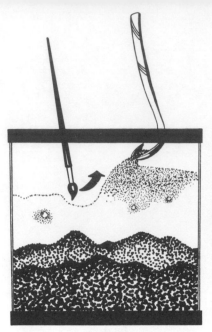

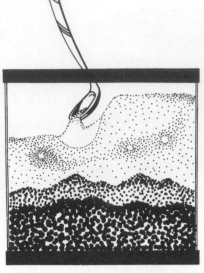

Brush out rounded impression at an angle. Pour mound to the right of it.

Fill hollow with yellow. Layer it against the sky.

Cover with sky.

If you wish, add a few streaks of white or gray for clouds as you build the sky. On an **area of** sky, brush away a rounded impression at an angle. Then pour a mound of sky on the surface to the right of the brushed-out section.

Fill the rounded, slightly tilted impression with yellow or white. Be sure that the yellow is also against the side of the mound on the right side. Cover with sky. Use the needle against the glass to push the right side of the moon into a rounded shape (up and over).

Use the eraser end of a pencil or any other similarly shaped instrument (ball-point pen end, the kind that is not retractable) to push the sky. This will cause the crescent to become deeper and the tips narrower. Check the illustration.

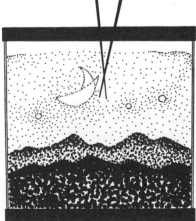

Use needle to push right side of moon up and over.

Use pencil end to further shape the crescent moon.

Finished moon in night sky.

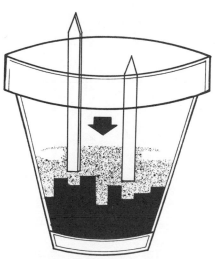

Night sky mixture

Layer of black

CITY SKYLINE

As an optional lesson, create a city skyline base for your night sky and moon. Since the techniques are the same as those learned in the geometric designs (especially the Indian blanket design), it should be fairly easy for you to execute these instructions.

Use a fairly tall container. Place a thick layer of black sand in the container bottom. Cover with sky. As you did with the Indian blanket design, use a square-ended instrument to press down the black base at irregular intervals for the building silhouettes.

Use plant stake to make square-bottomed impressions.

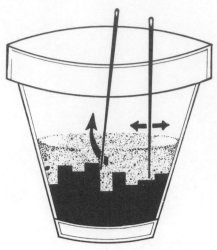

Use needle to make squares sharper.

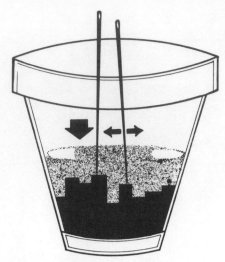

Correct the tops of the buildings
with the needle.

You can make the corners of the square impressions sharper by moving the needle against the glass in upward strokes, then running the needle across the top of each square if necessary. Then utilize the needle to poke into the black in several places to suggest more buildings. (Some of them could even be pointed on the top to suggest church steeples.) When you use the knitting needle to add buildings, make a series of pokes, one right next to the other, until a square area is filled with the night sky mixture.

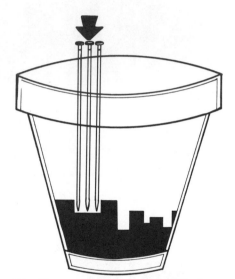

Use the needle in a series of strokes,
one next to the other, to make more
square impressions.

Finished city skyline silhouette.

BIRDS

The final lesson in skies will be the construction of birds. These are simple to do but will probably be one of the most important sand designs you have learned so far.

On a level area of sky, pour a small amount of white sand. The sand will naturally form a tapered mound. With the knitting needle, poke down into the center of the mound until there is a slight impression on the underside of the mound. You are now ready to cover the shape. It is very important that the bird is covered from behind, the spoon following a center to edge motion. These instruction insure the crispness of the bird, so that it will not flatten with the additional weight of the sky.

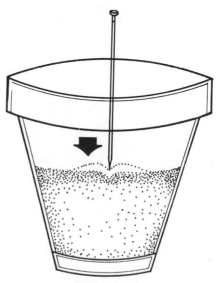

Pour mound of white.

Poke down.

SIDE VIEW
Cover mound.

Finished bird.

For variety, make the birds black or brown. To create a sea gull, add a bit of black at the tip of the white mound before poking.

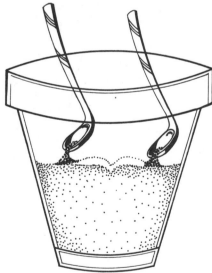

Add black tips on wing mounds
for sea gull.

Finished sea gull.

VI
GEO-GRAPHICS

MEADOWS, GRASSLANDS, AND TREE LINES

There are two ways of rendering a basic meadow. Color blending is an excellent method when done properly. Where a great deal of detail is not necessary, meadow areas can be constructed of blended shades of green. The color mixing is done the same way as with the ocean colors, using a lighter shade of green initially and progressing to medium and, finally, darker shades for perspective.

In cases where the foreground is an important part of the scene, it is advisable to intersperse some grassy areas. These areas may be portrayed as rows of grass, suggesting some ground level variation, or as clumps that are large in the foreground and diminish in size as they are added in the background.

To render rows of grass, begin by spooning in some light green. Over this, spoon some dark green in a rather thick layer; then cover the dark layer with more light green. With the upholstery needle, jab through the top layer of light green into the dark green, making the jagged row of grass. This technique is identical to the motion used in creating the crest of the ocean wave.

Blended meadow.

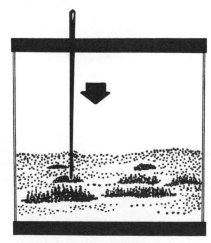

Poke layers of dark green for rows of grass.

Poke mounds of dark green for clumps.

Example of clumps and rows of grass. Perspective shown by difference in sizes.

Layer dark green on meadow base. Jab into dark green for tree line. Correct foothills after jabbing.

To make the clumps of grass, spoon a mound of dark green over the light-green base. Cover the dark mound with light green and jab the needle into the dark mound at different angles as shown in the illustration to create the spikes of grass. As was mentioned before, remember to make foreground clumps larger and the ones in the background smaller for perspective.

You may apply this same technique to invent other sand scenes, such as tree lines. Over a finished meadow base, spoon in a layer of dark green. Cover this layer with whatever color you have chosen for foothills. Make the foothill layer about one-quarter to one-half inch deep. Jab through the foothill to make the tree line. After the jagged tree line has been made, go back and add peaks over the foothill layer, of the same color of course, to correct and add to the clarity of the hill forms.

These additions add interest to the entire sand scene. Use your imagination for color variation.

PLAINS, PRAIRIES, AND DESERTS

Blended desert with streaks of tan and brown.

Use what you have already learned about color blending. All that is needed here are a few suggestions as to appropriate color mixes.

A desert, prairie, or plain is constructed by layering shades of beige, brown, and tan. If you wish, mix these colors first and then spoon them into place. Intersperse some streaks of tan and brown throughout the blend of beige to suggest varying ground levels. The streaky appearance is very important. Graduate to darker colors as you build up to the horizon line. If you wish, position a few clumps of grass to suggest desert vegetation for interest.

CACTUS

A desert would not be complete without the addition of a few cacti.

Begin by spooning in about one inch of blended desert base. Over a level area of desert, spoon a mound of dark green. With the knitting needle, push the green down through the beige. You may

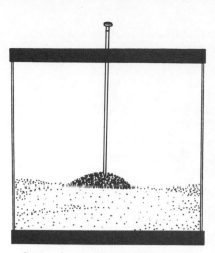

Spoon in mound of dark green.
Position needle.

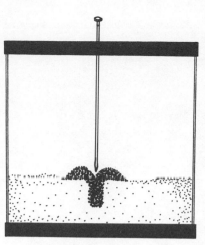

Poke down knitting needle
twice if necessary.

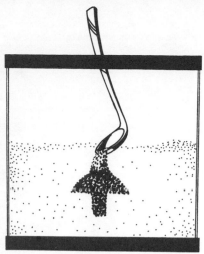

Pour second mound of green.
Cover with background.

have to poke down more than one time to achieve the desired thickness for the cactus' main upright trunk. Spoon another dark green mound in the same place as the initial mound was positioned. Cover all with the beige blend.

Use the size one knitting needle to poke through the beige sand and into the green mound on each side of the stem, creating three rough "arms" for the cactus. The middle, upright arm will be formed fairly well at this point; the side arms will need some correction. Use the upholstery needle against the glass to bring the side mounds up. The illustration shows the needle positioning.

Cacti are not perfectly symmetrical, so if the arms of the cactus are a bit uneven, do not be concerned. If desired, you may make some two-armed cacti. Let your sense of design govern what you do.

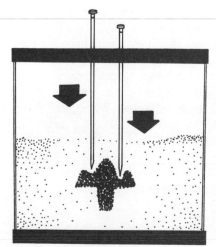

Poke twice,
forming center arm of cactus.

Shape sides of cactus.
Position each arm separately.

Completed scene.

SHADED HILLS

Since the pouring techniques for foothills and mountains have been previously explained and illustrated, there should be little need for more detail at this point. If you are still having difficulty with hills, reread the sections on islands and foothills. Remember to maintain the pivot point as you pour and there should be no problem.

To add more dimension and realism to your elementary foothills, direct your efforts towards achieving a three-dimensional effect. You will find that browsing through travel brochures, photography magazines, and even picture calendars will give you new ideas. Combine your skills and techniques and apply your knowledge to create different design schemes. Your proficiency will increase with practice. A sense of perspective and depth awareness will also come naturally with time. These two factors are extremely important if you wish to achieve perfection in renderings of landscapes and seascapes.

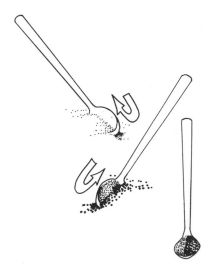

*Position two colors of sand
on the spoon by dipping
each side into a color separately.*

Shaded hills and mountains will greatly enhance a basic meadow, desert, or island motif. Choose two contrasting, but similar colors (i.e., brown and tan, black and beige, gray and dark blue). It may be easier to first try this technique using a tablespoon. The iced-tea spoon is narrower and may initially be tedious to handle in this particular lesson. It would be helpful to practice a few hills to get the feel of the sand flow.

On the spoon, place two shades of sand, one on each side. It may be helpful at first to use a second spoon to position the sand, but you should try to dip the spoon into each color, one side at a time, without spilling or mixing the sands. Approximate the amounts on each side so that they are equal. If there is more of one color than the other, the hill will not be evenly shaded.

After this preparation, position the spoon tip toward you directly over the place in the scene where the shaded hill is to fall. Gently tilt the spoon. As the sand falls, the mound will be bi-colored, one side darker than the other. It may be helpful to move the spoon from side to side slightly as you pour with the tip toward you.

These hills have a tendency to crest in a rounded shape. It may be necessary to sharpen the peak. Do this by applying both colors in their respective positions. Shaded mountains and foothills are a sure eye-catcher. Next we will be discussing snow-capped mountains: try making a shaded mountain of white and light blue or gray. Keep this idea in mind.

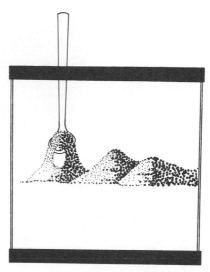

Spoon facing you, pour sand into a bi-colored mound. Slight sideways motion is used.

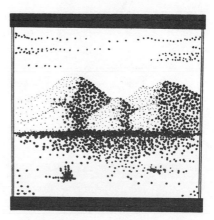

Finished three-dimensional mountains and foothills.

SNOW-CAPPED MOUNTAINS

Recall what you have learned as you combined different colors for contrast and authenticity. For color variation—and to achieve definition between the black, low-altitude mountains and the snow-capped, higher peaks—mix purple and dark blue, or purple with black, dark blue with black, etc., for the base color of the higher mountains. Pour large mounds of this mixture over your final row of low mountains (formed in black).

Think back a moment to the volcano lesson. As you added the red, a dip or impression was made on the crest of the base mound with the tip of the spoon. Here we will follow the same procedure, substituting white sand for red. Make a

Top mountain with white, making dip with tip of spoon as you pour.

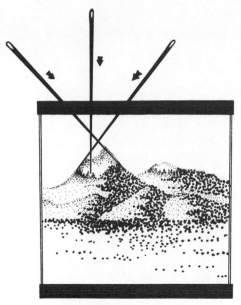

Jab white into the mountain top as shown.

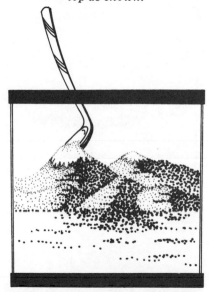

Recap peak with white after jabbing.

Finished snow-covered mountains with setting sun and birds.

small dip with the tip of the spoon as you pour, allowing the peak to hold more white on the very top and preventing the white from running down the sides of the mound.

Continue to build the complete mountain by using the upholstery needle to jab the white into the mound. Jab gently, holding the needle upright for the center area and at angles parallel to the mountain's respective sides.

Add the finishing touch by applying more white on the misshapen crest of the mountain, forming a crisp peak. Neatness counts!

Further enhance the design by adding a setting sun, clouds, and birds to create a more aesthetic rendition.

LAKES AND MARSHLANDS

Layer dark green over meadow base. Cover with blue water mixture.

Use the skills you have acquired in creating rows and clumps of grass, along with some layering techniques, for this lesson. Follow the instructions carefully as the layers and subsequent jabbing are done.

Construct a base of blended greens for the meadow. Mix some shades of blue for the lake.

Over the blended meadow base, place a layer of dark green. Over this, spoon a layer of the blue mix. Jab through the blue into the green, to suggest the tall grass that grows around water areas. Layer more blue over the jabbed blue. On each side of this blue addition, mound a bit of light green.

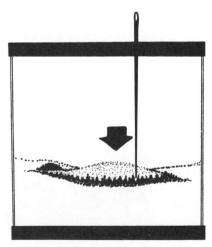

Jab into dark green for grass.
Add more water.
Add side mounds of meadow color.

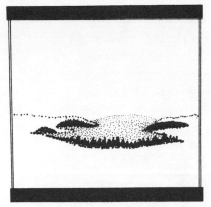

Layer-in dark green.
Cover green with meadow
color and water as indicated.

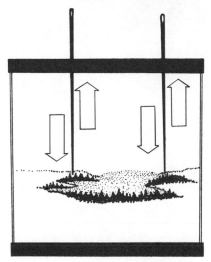

Jab through the water and the
meadow colors to the dark green.

On the two side mounds of light green, layer a bit more dark green. Spoon in more blue until it is up to the level of the dark green—overlapping some of the dark green with the blue. Cover any exposed dark green with light green.

Jab through the light green and blue into the dark green, creating the grass blades.

Continue by adding a bit more blue over the area where the jabbing was done. Layer some dark green over the blue and cover it with light green. Jab the light green into the dark green to finish making the bordering grass.

You may increase the size of the lake or marsh after you have tried this initial exercise. Remember to build the dark green over the light green, then add blue, jab, add more blue and dark green, and jab. Continue building with light green, dark green and blue, jabbing as necessary. Add some white streaks to the blue if you wish.

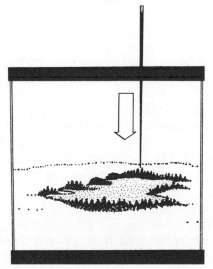

Add more blue and cover with dark
green. Cover all with meadow color.
Jab again as shown.

Finished lake or marshland with
bordering grasses.

SNOW SCENES

Stormy sky of streaky gray, blue, and white color blend.

Make a basic landscape using a different color scheme to render a snow scene. Mix gray and pale blue with white to make soft, rolling hills of snow. Sparkle sand will further enhance this landscape. If none is available, mix a bit of silver aluminum glitter with some white sand for a glistening effect. Layer this glitter-mixed sand over each hill for definition. Intersperse some tufts of grass showing through the snow. Build a tree line and snow-capped mountains to complete the scene. Since color blending is so important here, concentrate on varying contrasts. The basic techniques of building any landscape apply here, so step-by-step instruction should not be necessary. Remember to make a cloud-filled stormy sky over this winter scene.

WINDING ROADS AND PATHS

Construction of a road or path is just a carefully planned succession of mounds and layers. Here, it is important to keep perspective in mind. As you build up the path in the container, gradually diminish its width to give the illusion of distance. Choose a background color; light green is a good base on which to build a brown road.

Begin by mounding the light green on one side of the container, leaving the other side of the container bottom uncovered. Over the initial mound, spoon a layer of brown that is wide at the bottom and gradually narrows as it reaches the crest of the green. Do not extend the brown over the crest of the green; place it just against the slope.

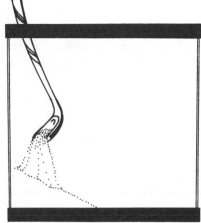

Mound meadow color on one side of the container.

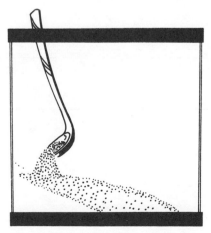

Layer brown over mound up to the crest but not extending over it.

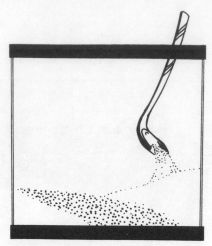

Cover brown with light green as shown.

Mound light green over the brown layer so that there is a slope up to the opposite container wall. Leave the top of the brown layer exposed.

Now spoon brown over the light green, connecting the top of the first brown layer with the bottom of this new addition.

Cover the new section of road with more light green, sloping up to the first side of the container this time, to provide a base for an extension of the road.

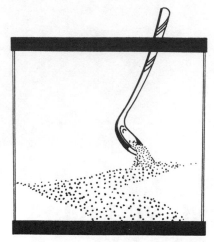

Pour brown layer over green, connecting the two brown layers.

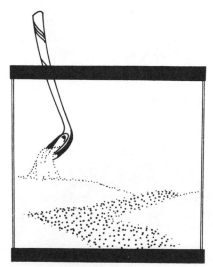

Cover brown with background as before.

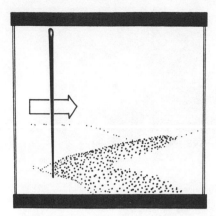

Round off corner with needle.

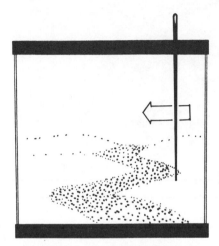

Layer in more brown and cover.
Round off corner as before.

Use the upholstery needle against the glass to round off the corner where the two brown layers meet. Again layer some brown over the green mound, cover it, and correct the corner again.

You may now use the needle against the glass to make the last section of the path more upright.

Complete the design by building a tree line and mountains. By making the path gradually narrower, you will make it appear to diminish into the hills and forest.

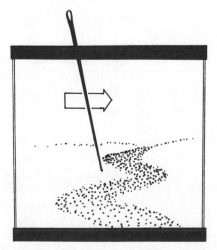

Correct last section of path as indicated.

Completed design with path fading into the background.

STREAMS

Layer dark green over light green and cover with water.

Streams are constructed by following the same technique as for the road. Of course, you will want to substitute a blue mixture in place of the brown, and you may streak some white through the blue. As you construct the stream you may want to form some grass at its edge. Do this by layering dark green over the light-green base before the water color is positioned. Jab through the blue into the dark green. Cover the blue water with dark green and then the background light green. Jab the dark green to form streamside grass on the opposite bank. Continue in this manner until the stream is complete.

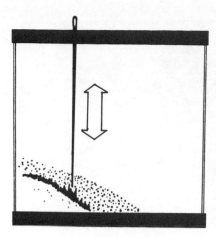

Jab dark green.

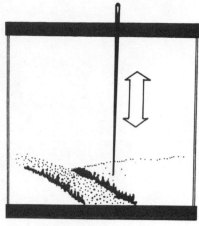

Layer dark green over water and cover with meadow color. Jab.

Stream completed with grassy banks.

Of course you may also place grass along the road or path edge in the same manner.

As an additional point of interest, with the brush make some notches in the water area and fill with black to create rocks.

Follow instructions for stream, adding rocks as explained.

Example of stream with rocks.

WATERFALLS

Build a stream or lake up to the horizon line, to provide a base for a waterfall. If you follow the directions carefully, this lesson should be easy, since you have already learned to shape upright forms.

At the top of a lake or stream, position a large foothill at each side. Be sure that the slopes of these hills do not fully cover the water. Place them so that they are at least one-half inch apart, leaving the water exposed between the hills. In this area, spoon alternate layers or mounds of blue and white. Build the height of the foothills as you are mounding the blue and white. Any misplaced sand will be corrected later.

Use the upholstery needle to jab through the blue and white sands to blur them for the falling water effect. If some of the surrounding hills fall away as you are jabbing, spoon more hill color into position.

Position two large hills ½ inch apart.

Layer-in blue and white.

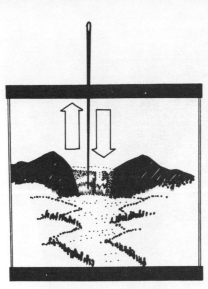

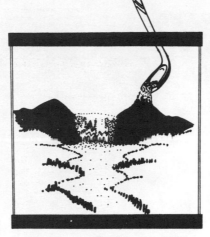

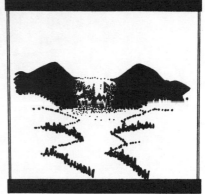

Jab into blue and white.

Add water and additional hills as necessary.

Example of waterfall before shaping.

When the jabbing and hill positioning are complete, you are ready to use the needle to shape the waterfall (as was done for the lighthouse). Holding the needle against the glass, use an upward stroke to bring the water colors into an upright position. After the shaping is complete, use the artist's brush to remove any brown that might have fallen over the blue and white sands while the shaping took place. Correct the hill peaks by spooning more hill color into place to repeak them. To further enhance the scene, build a rather large mountain over the waterfall. It will appear to be in the distance behind the waterfall.

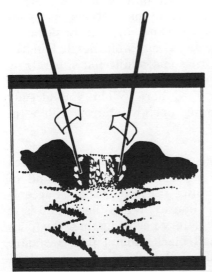

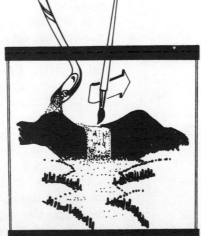

Shape waterfall as indicated.

Use brush to remove any overlapping brown and correct hills if needed.

Completed waterfall with background as shown.

SIMPLE HOUSE OR BUILDING

A small house that can be added to many different scenes is a good point of interest. After you have mastered these instructions, use your imagination to improve and vary this basic building. Render it to be a log cabin nestled in the mountains, or with some additional superstructure, create a barn in a farm scene. Use the information described here. What you already know about forming upright shapes will be of value.

On a meadow base, place a small mound of black sand. Cover the black with a large mound of brown or red or white (any color that is acceptable to you for the house). When the mound is in place, use the upholstery needle against the glass to shape the small black mound into a square for the door. After the shaping is complete, spoon more brown over the entire form, making the mound larger on the right side of the door.

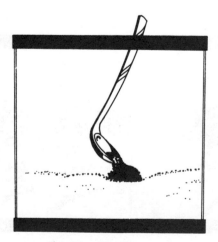

Position black mound.

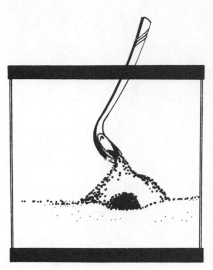

Cover with brown.

Shape black into door with needle.

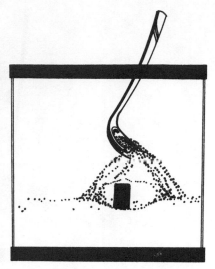

Cover gently, making brown mound larger on the right.

At one side of the black square door, where you built up the brown mound with additional sand, brush out a notch. (Try to make the bottom of the notch fairly level as you will be squaring it off for a window.) Fill this notch with black. Cover the window with more brown. Use the upholstery needle to shape the window (black) into a square. Do this the same way as the door was done. After shaping the window, cover the entire brown form, which now has a door and a window, with more brown. (The mound will be misshapen, which necessitates covering it.)

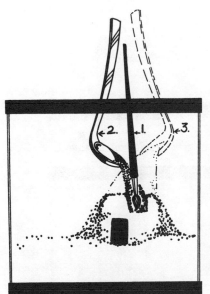

1. *Brush away notch.*
2. *Spoon in black.*
3. *Cover with brown.*

Use needle to shape window.

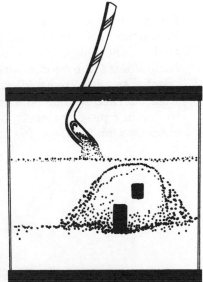

Add to the brown mound as needed. Cover rough house with background.

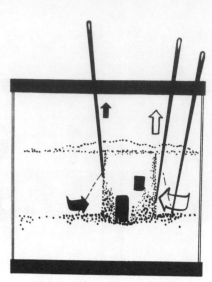

Use needle as indicated to shape house walls.

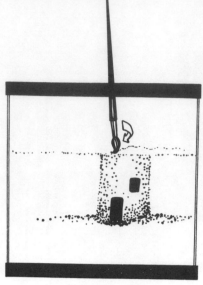

Level off top.

Now cover the brown mound with background. You may use a background of sky mixture or, if you intend the house to sit in the middle of a meadow, cover it with more meadow mixture. Straighten the sides of the house with the upholstery needle, as shown. Use the artist's brush to remove excess background sand (brush towards the middle of the container), exposing the top of the house and making it level.

Finally, pour a peaked mound of black over the brown house to form a roof. Cover all with the background, making sure to pour some sand on each side of the roof mound first, then pouring "center to edge" to complete the covering. Shape with the needle against the glass, if necessary, to further peak the roof and make it neat. Add chimneys and gables for variety.

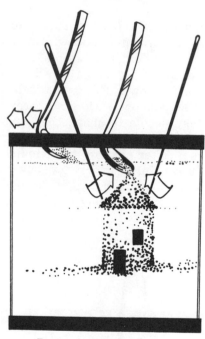

Pour roof mound. Shape after covering with background.

Finished house or simple building.

VII
GROWING THINGS: FLOWERS AND TREES

Make V shape with mounding technique and brush.

Spoon in tapered layer of dark green.

Cover, maintaining the V.

BASIC FLOWER

The type of flower that you will learn to create here is easy and fun to do. Employ your basic jabbing techniques. Use bright colors for the petal area.

Pour a background (white) in two mounds on opposite sides of the container. Make them high enough so that there is a deep *V* shape created. Over the slopes of this indentation, spoon (in a sloping layer) dark green. This green will eventually be the bottom leaves of the flower. Make each slope of green in the *V* shape slightly thicker in its center, tapering at the ends, so that the leaves will be more realistic. Cover the first layer of green with more background, again in a *V* shape. This *V* must be maintained throughout the design. Over the background, spoon more green as before and cover it again with background. (Maintain *V*!)

After all the leaf layers are in place and have been covered with background, you will be ready to form the flower stem. In the center of the *V* spoon a mound of dark green. Use the size one knitting needle to poke down through all the layers in the center area to create a stem. It may be necessary to do this twice, but normally one poke should be sufficient.

The flower petals are next constructed by placing three or more mounded layers of brightly colored sand within the *V* formed by the background. As you progress, it may be necessary to build

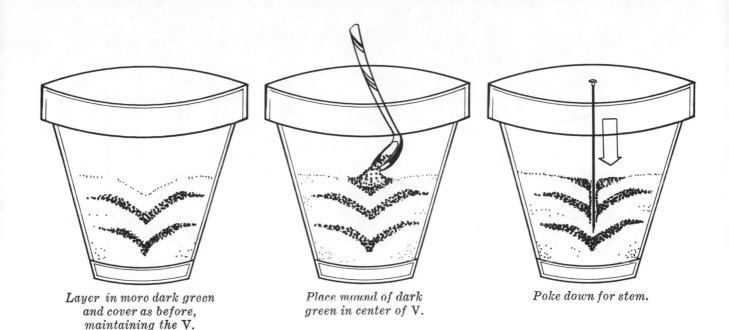

Layer in more dark green
and cover as before,
maintaining the V.

Place mound of dark
green in center of V.

Poke down for stem.

background height at the sides to keep the *V*
deep enough to contain the flower petal colors.
Use your own judgment. If you choose to add
more background, be careful that you do not
pour any background over or into these brightly
colored mounds. (Color suggestion: use red,
yellow, and orange, or pink, red, and purple.)
When the mounds are in place, cover all with
background. Achieve a level surface this time.
Now use the size one knitting needle to poke
through the petal colors only, at angles, to form
the petal leaves. Use the illustration for a guide
to needle positioning.

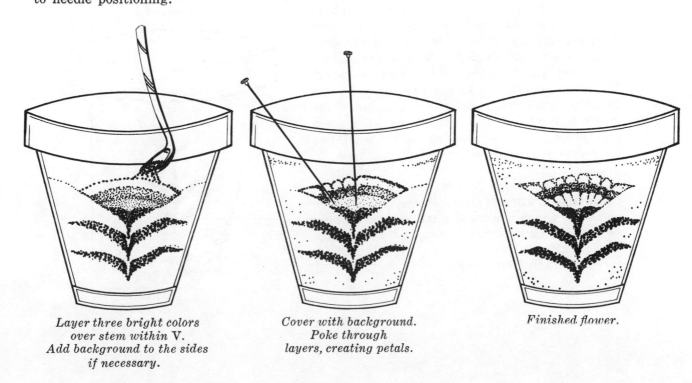

Layer three bright colors
over stem within V.
Add background to the sides
if necessary.

Cover with background.
Poke through
layers, creating petals.

Finished flower.

Form the leaves as before.
Make them lower on the stem.

Place mound for
the stem in center of
the background V.

TULIPS

Tulips are even easier than the basic flower if you apply your shaping skills. Form the leaves in the same manner as for the basic flower, but place the two green bottom layers a bit closer together. Tulips typically have their long blade-like leaves at the base of the stem rather than along its entire length.

After the stem has been formed, mound some red into the *V*-shaped indentation. Add enough to make the level of the red even across the indentation, not peaked. Cover this with background. With the needle against the glass, bring the sides of the red up so that the red is more cup-shaped. Using the number five knitting needle, poke into the top of the flower shape to make the tooth-like petals of the tulip. You may, if you wish, use a thinner needle and shape each pointed petal. Use your own judgment, but try both methods.

Both of these basic flowers can be applied to many design schemes. Try a Pennsylvania Dutch motif in which you will have several flowers around the entire container topped with a geometric pattern. You may also incorporate miniature flowers in a landscape.

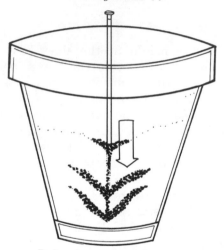

Poke stem mound down.

Fill the V-shaped area above
stem with red sand.

Use the upholstery needle to
make the top of the
tulip more cup-shaped.

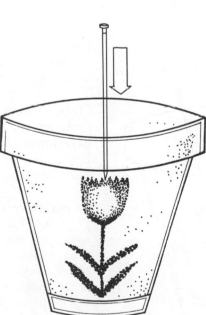

Form the petals of the
tulip with a knitting needle.

Optional method:
Shape each petal individually
with the upholstery needle.

MUSHROOMS

Use your skills to create a mushroom shape that can be added to a landscape, or fashion a single mushroom in the container.

Choose a background color and spoon it into the container to provide a base. Build a mound of dark brown for the mushroom's stem and cover it with the base color. Use the needle against the glass to shape the mound into a stem.

Brush away some of the background, exposing the top of the stem and creating a slight depression approximately two inches long. Across this area, spoon a thin layer of black sand. Over this black, spoon a mound of yellow and cover that with another layer of black thicker than the initial layer. Poke the black through the yellow at close intervals to make the mushroom's gills. Use the upholstery needle.

Pour mound for the stem.

Shape stem with the needle.

114

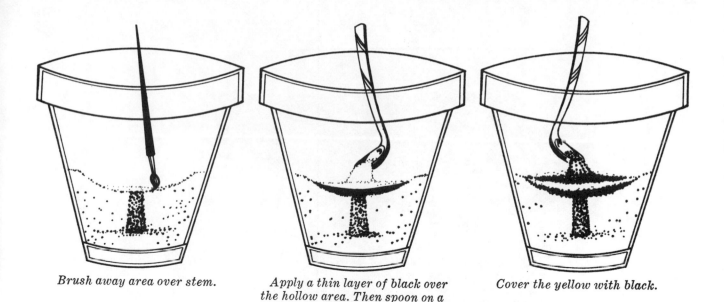

Brush away area over stem.

Apply a thin layer of black over the hollow area. Then spoon on a mound of yellow.

Cover the yellow with black.

After the poking is completed, it will be necessary to correct the top black layer, which will become uneven from poking. Use the brush or simply spoon some extra black over the uneven surface to make it smooth. For the cap of the mushroom, spoon a large mound of tan or brown sand. The natural flow of the sand will form a gently sloping mound. For interest, you may want to brush out some notches within the cap area and fill them with a bright color, covering these with tan (or brown) as you progress, to make a spotted top.

Poke into the black for the mushroom's gills.

Pour a cap on the gill area and cover all.

Finished mushroom. Spotted top used for variety.

BASIC TREES

A basic shade tree is little more than a mushroom with a different top. Create a tree trunk in the same manner as the mushroom stem was made. Check back to the mushroom section if you have any trouble.

Brush away the background from the area over the trunk top. Add sand on each side to form a cup-shape in which to pour some dark green. Fill the cup. Use the needle to poke in a haphazard manner, achieving an irregularly shaped tree top. (At this point, you will be forming only the bottom half of the tree top.)

Over the bottom tree-top section, pour more dark green in a mound and cover it with background. Then proceed as before, using the needle against the glass and jabbing to form the top section of the tree.

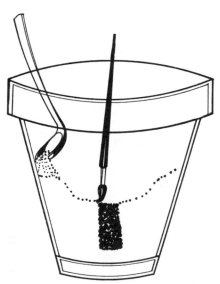

Brush away background after you have constructed the trunk, to create a hollow for the tree top.

Fill the hollow with green and use the needle to make the tree top irregular and slightly blurred for realism. Build up the background at the sides of the tree top. Add more dark green over the bottom half of the tree top. Build up the background as necessary to stabilize the green area.

Add more dark green over the bottom half of the tree top. Build up the background adjoining the green area as much as is needed to stabilize it.

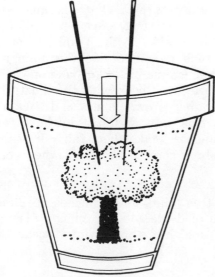

Use the needle to shape the tree top after you have covered it with background.

Create the tree trunk as before. Brush away background to expose the top of the tree trunk. Leave background mounds on each side.

Layer-in some dark brown over background mounds.

Pour background over end sections of branches.

BRANCHED TREES

Construct a basic trunk following the same instructions as in the previous lesson. After you have brushed away the background and exposed the top of the tree trunk, leave a mound of background on each side of the trunk; layer some brown on each mound beside the main trunk. Place another mound of background on each end section of brown. (Check with the illustration.) Continue adding brown layers and background mounds in this manner until you have formed several branches. Make them fairly long as you will be pushing some parts away when you add the leaves.

When the tree trunk and branches are finished, you will be ready to add the foliage. (Try using bare trunk and limbs in a winter scene for an interesting effect.)

Layer-in some more brown, filling cavity of main trunk as well as adding branches.

Cover and continue to layer brown and background to form more branches. Cover with background to the level shown.

Spoon in dark green over branched area.

Layer some dark green over the branch area. With the number one knitting needle, poke the dark green down around the forked branches. With the needle, shape the green as necessary to make the tree realistic. You may have to add more green as you go along to make the foliage full enough. When the side foliage looks correct, place more green over the tree top and cover with background. Then proceed to shape the top of the tree into its final form with the upholstery needle.

Use size one knitting needle to poke green down around the branches.

Add more green over area shown.

Cover the final green layer with background and use the needle to shape tree top.

PALM TREES

We will describe a leaning palm tree in this lesson. If you want an upright one, follow the instructions for the cactus stem to form the trunk and then proceed to make the fronds on the top as they are described here.

Prepare an island or desert base at the bottom of the container. The palm will begin at the horizon line, so add a sloping mound of sky color to one side of the container; this will form a base upon which the leaning trunk of the palm can be poured.

Against the slope of the sky, spoon some brown sand, thicker at the bottom and tapering as you approach the top. Over the brown, spoon a thin layer of black and poke it into the brown slightly to suggest bark. Use the upholstery needle. Correct the uneven surface of black by adding just a very thin layer over the poked surface. Cover the trunk with sky.

Layer brown over a mound of sky.
Cover that with a thin layer of black.

Sky level

Poke the black into the brown trunk
to suggest bark.
Add sky to the left of trunk.

120

Mound sky on each side of the trunk.

Pour dark green over the sky area.

Jab dark green for the fronds of the tree. Add more green over the jabbed frond surface to create a smooth, curved surface.

Be sure that the sky is built up slightly to each side of the trunk. This will provide a base upon which to pour the green fronds. You may use the brush if you wish to create a more exact base. Over the sky, on each side of the trunk, place a mound of dark green. Jab through the green to form the jagged palm fronds. Correct the top surfaces of the fronds so that they will be smooth. When you have completed these, cover them with sky.

If you wish, add a second layer of fronds, using the same instructions. After these fronds are completed, cover them with sky. It may be necessary to use the knitting needle to poke down in the center of these fronds in order to connect them with the trunk. Use this finished tree to enhance an island motif.

Cover the initial fronds with sky mixture.

Add a second layer of fronds if desired. Follow the same instructions as before.

Cover the tree top with sky and use the knitting needle to poke through the center area to connect the fronds with the trunk.

EVERGREEN TREES

Use this tree type in any woodland scene as well as for holiday designs.

Begin by forming a short trunk, using the same methods that were employed in the mushroom stem and tree trunk. Brush away the background over the trunk area so that there is a level area approximately two inches long. On this level area, spoon a mound of dark green and cover it with background sand. Use the upholstery needle to shape the mound's slopes so that the degree of the angle is about the same on each side. Level the top area when shaping is complete.

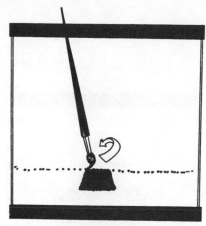

Form trunk; brush away background to expose trunk.

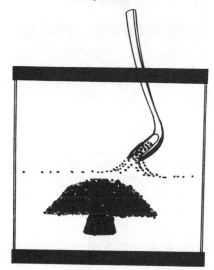

Spoon in green mound and cover.

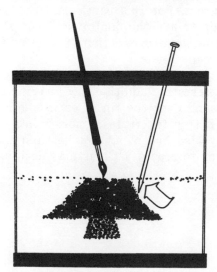

Shape tree sides and level top with brush.

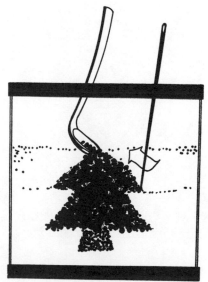

Pour second mound of green and cover. Shape sides again.

Level top area.

*Pour third mound and cover; shape
as before but peak top instead
of leveling it. Finished evergreen tree.*

On this new level, spoon a dark green mound smaller than the previous one. Cover it and shape as before. Brush away a level area on the crest of the mound.

You have the option of making the tree with as many or as few levels (boughs) as you want. Be sure to reduce the mounds into smaller sizes as you progress. For this particular tree, you are now ready to add the final mound and shape it. Follow the same instructions but peak the top of the green. Cover.

For an interesting addition, try layering a bit of sparkle sand over the tip of each bough of the evergreen tree to create a more wintry flavor. You may also brush out notches and fill them with color to create a Christmas design.

VIII
THE ANIMAL WORLD

BUTTERFLIES

Add a background color and brush away two indentations.

Butterflies provide a good design scheme by themselves; when combined in a meadow scene, in miniature renditions of course, they will add a bright note of color and interest. Their construction is easily achieved, as it is merely the clever mounding of bright colors.

Begin by building a foundation (use white for this lesson) in which you will make two indentations. You can make these indentations with the brush or with the spoon tip, scooping out the valleys if this seems faster. Choose three bright colors (purple, pink, and yellow, or orange, red, and yellow). Within these indentations, layer the three colors, mounding them slightly as shown in the illustration. Be sure to align the crest of each mound with the bottom of each indentation. When the mounds are properly positioned, apply some background over the outside slope of each mound (not over the inside slopes). Position the background so that an incline is created beside each outside slope.

Repeat the mounding of the three colors (as was done for the bottom wings) for the top set of wings. Cover the outside slopes of the wings with background as before to stabilize the colorful wing layers. In the center of the indentation between the top set of wings, place at least one spoonful of black sand. Use the size one knitting needle to push the black sand down the center of the wings for the butterfly's body. Poke far enough so that the black extends below the wings into the background. You will probably have to

Mound three colors within the indentations. Align the colors so that the crests and bottoms of the mounds are in the same position (indicated by arrows).

Add inclined background on each side. Correct top layer of color if necessary.

Follow the same instructions to form the top set of wings. Cover outside edges with background to stabilize the wings.

poke twice to achieve a thick enough body. Be sure to follow the same exact path when you poke the second time. If necessary, spoon some additional black in the center indentation, over the body, to remain in a mound for the butterfly's head. Leave any black sand that remains lying over the wing slopes to suggest antennae. Cover everything now with background and shape the head a bit with the needle as necessary.

Mound black in center of indentation.

Use the needle to poke black down through the center of the wings for the body of the butterfly. You may have to poke twice for thickness. Add more black if it is necessary.

Add more black for head. Cover with background and shape head, leaving any excess for antennae.

BUMBLEBEES

A bumblebee, like flowers and butterflies, can be the center of attention when used singly in a container; done on a smaller scale, it can accentuate a flower/meadow scene.

In a background color, create a long, half-oval indentation, and immediately to the left of that impression make another half-round hollow. Use the artist's brush for this preliminary shaping. Into the oval hollow, mound some yellow for the body of the bee. Into the rounded one, mound black for the bee's head. Use the upholstery needle to poke through the black (near the right side of the black mound), creating some legs for the bee. Layer black on the background surface near the head for antennae. Then, correct the black mound by adding a bit more black sand to round it off. As you are doing this, spoon some black in a thin layer over the top of the yellow mound; use the upholstery needle to poke the black down into the yellow at intervals for the bee's striped body. Remove any excess black from the yellow mound's surface.

*Brush away two hollows—
one large oval and one round.*

Mound black and yellow as indicated.

128

Extend thin layer of black over background. Poke down legs as shown.

Correct the head and add a layer of black over the yellow mound. Poke for bee's stripes.

Remove any excess black from the yellow mound's surface. Cover the head and the rear portion of the body with background mounds sloping as shown. Leave center area over body exposed.

Now cover the bee's head and the rear portion of the body with sloping background mounds, leaving the center area of the bee's body exposed. Against the rear slope of background, mound some white so that it contacts the body. Cover this mound with a thin layer of gray. Add a second layer of white over this gray divisional line, creating two wings. Cover all with background for the finished bee.

After covering body as described, mound white against rear slope as shown.

Cover the white with thin layer of gray and continue by adding a second layer of white for the top wing.

Cover all. Finished bee.

OWLS

Create an owl perched on a branch in a night scene for an interesting sand subject. You may incorporate this design in a woodland scene where the foreground might be a close-up view of a large tree. Build the owl shape by beginning with the tail, which appears below the branch.

On a level background surface, mound some tan. Poke with a size one knitting needle until a square, feathered shape results. Level the top of the square and the background. Spoon a layer of black over the tail.

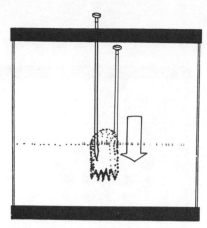

Mound tan and poke for owl's tail.

On the left end of the black, mound a bit of background and over this layer add more black, creating a branched tree limb. On the branch, put two small mounds of orange above the tail, about one-quarter inch apart. Use the needle (size one) to poke down two talons (claws) in each mound. Mound some background over each end of the branch, each mound sloping toward the bird's feet, leaving about one inch of branch still exposed. Over the owl's feet, mound a fairly large quantity of tan.

Add more background up to the level of the tan mound's crest in preparation for shaping. Use the upholstery needle to shape the tan mound into an oval-shaped body. (Refer to the section on sun shaping if you need detailed instructions for round shaping.) Use the brush to level off the entire surface.

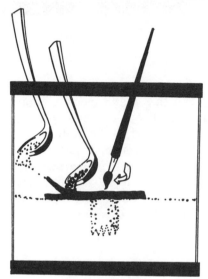

Layer-in branch.
Create branch end as indicated.
Level off.

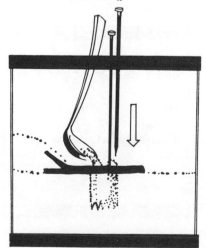

Mound two small quantities of orange. Poke down for the owl's feet.

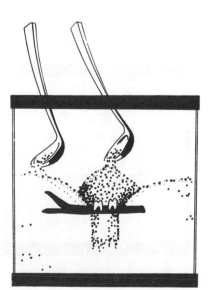

Mound background on each side. Leave 1 inch of branch exposed. Mound tan in exposed area.

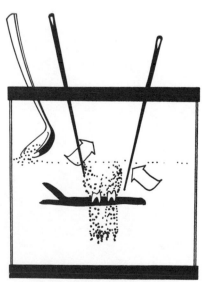

Add more background and shape the body.

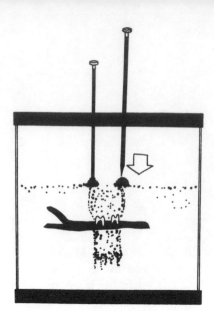

On the level surface place two black mounds and poke down on each side of owl's body.

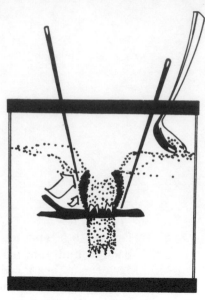

Reshape body. Add background to form foundation for owl's head.

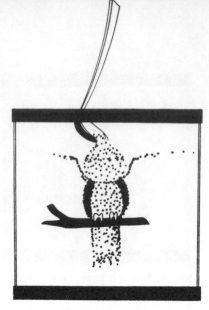

Mound brown for the head.

Over each side of the tan body, spoon a mound of black sand. With the size one needle, poke the black down on each side next to the body to form wings. After this is done, you may need to correct the sides of the owl's body for neatness. Add some background on each side of the body. Over the body (between the background mounds), spoon a mound of brown for the owl's head.

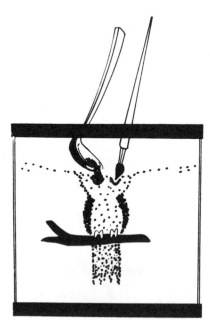

Brush out notches and add black for eyes.

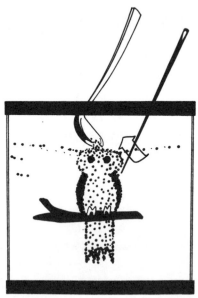

Cover eyes and shape head. (Build background as needed.)

Brush out two notches into which you will spoon some black for the owl's eyes. Cover the black eyes with brown and shape them if necessary. They need not be perfectly round. Add background on the sides as needed in order to stabilize the head shape. After the background is in place, use the needle to round off the sides of the head.

On the surface of the head, spoon a mound of black. Use the size one knitting needle to poke down through the center of the owl's face between the eyes to the bottom of the head. Poke as much as you think necessary to form a triangular nose and beak area as shown in the illustration. Use the brush to level the top of the head (the black portion). As you brush, leave the ends of the level black area at an upward angle for the owl's horns. Cover all with background.

Mound black on head surface.
Poke down for detail in owl's face.

Level top of head, leaving ends
of black at an upward angle
for the horns of the owl.

Cover all.
Finished owl.

DUCKS

Construct a duck within a lake scene for a touch of color and interest. On a level area of water, brush out an impression half oval in shape. Into this impression, spoon some white so that there is a slight mound created above the water surface. Brush out a hollow in the center of the mound. Spoon a thin layer of black or gray against the surface of the hollow. Cover this with white so that there is a mound created over the present water level. Make the mound a bit higher on the left side to provide enough sand to form the duck's neck.

Brush out hollow on water surface.

Fill with white.

Brush out hollow and layer-in black or gray against curved surface.

Cover the white mound with water, leaving the crest on the left side of the mound exposed. Use the needle in a long sweeping motion (toward the right) to shape the duck's back into a gentle curve. Move the needle against the inclined neck for clarity. Locate the needle behind the white form and push to the left slightly to force the duck's tail over and up. The duck's tail feathers should extend above the back level.

Cover with white, making left side of the mound slightly higher.

Cover with water and use needle in both directions to form the back and neck.

Push on tail section to shape.

135

Spoon small mound of white for head.

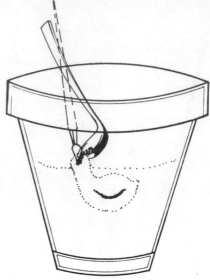

Add eye. Refer to whale eye instructions if you need help.

Over the exposed neck mound, spoon some additional white (pour mound slightly to the left of the neck) for the duck's head. This same procedure was used to make the firebird's head in the geometric lessons. Brush out a very small notch and spoon some black into it for the duck's eye. Cover this with white. (Be careful not to add too much.) In front of the head mound (on the left), spoon a small bit of yellow for the duck's bill. Cover the head section with "water." Use the needle against the glass to round off the head and make any necessary corrections.

Spoon small amount of yellow for bill.

Cover and use needle to shape head.

Dotted line indicates former water level. Pour additional white mound and surround with background (water).

Use needle to shape longer neck.

SWANS

You may create a swan by following the duck instructions up to the point where the neck mound is exposed. Simply add white sand over this mound, cover it on both sides, and use the needle to shape the longer neck. The head would be essentially the same with the exception of making a black bill instead of a yellow one.

Continue by adding the head, as before, after the long neck is formed. These birds are a graceful addition to any lake in a country scene.

Finished swan.

HORSES

Now that you have some basic animal shapes to add to your land and waterscapes, study the steps in the construction of the horse carefully.

On a level meadow area, spoon a mound of brown. Use the size one knitting needle to poke down four legs. Use the illustration as a guide for positioning. You may find it necessary to position legs differently for different animals. Add some more brown if it is needed as you poke the legs down. To the left of the leg structure, spoon a mound of background. Build up the animal's body over the legs so that you will be able to add background around the form as you progress. On the rump area of the horse, add a bit more brown than you placed over the legs or back area. Add a bit of background on the right next to the rump. On this level, layer some black. This will be the horse's tail.

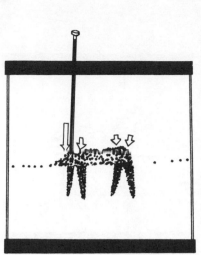

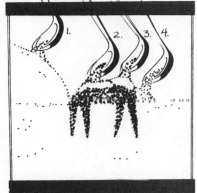

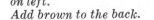

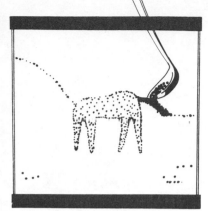

Mound brown and use needle to poke down legs.

1. *Pour mound of background on left.*
2. *Add brown to the back.*
3. *Add larger amount of brown for rump.*
4. *Add background to right of rump.*

Layer-in tail.

On the left, over the slope of background, layer some brown for the horse's neck. Be sure that it is thicker where it connects with the body area, tapering at the top of the neck. Now cover the back with background up to the point where the neck and body meet. Use the needle in a sweeping motion to make the back and rump curved. Over the neck spoon a layer of black for the mane.

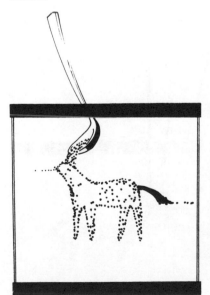

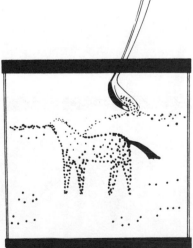

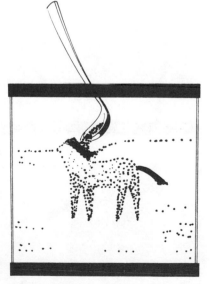

Spoon layer of brown for neck.

Spoon background over back as indicated.

Spoon mane over neck and against the background.

Spoon brown mound for head on leveled background.

Use needle to poke head into place.

Brush away a level area in the background sand on the left side of the neck. On this level area spoon a mound of brown sand and push it down with the size five knitting needle to shape the horse's head (similar to the cactus stem). Brush out a notch into which you will spoon some black for the horse's eye. Cover the eye with brown to form the head.

Brush away a level area on the background near head to correct any misplaced brown sand and to provide a foundation for the ear. Spoon a small bit of brown for the ear and cover with background. Use the upholstery needle to correct the head if necessary for clarity and definition.

Brush away notch for eye.

Fill in eye and cover with brown. Level background and layer-in ear of horse.

Cover head with background after ear is in place. Use needle to shape head. Make any other corrections.

DEER, CAMELS, AND SHEEP

From this one lesson you should, at this point, be able to expand upon the basic four-legged pattern to create deer and even camels. The deer would not have a mane or tail but would have antlers. Use the branched-tree lesson on a smaller scale over the head area for the final result. Combine the deer with a meadow or woodland scene. The net result will be a sure topic of conversation.

Example of finished deer.

Example of finished camel.

For a camel, follow the horse pattern until the body is formed. Make a thin rope-like tail. On the horse's back, spoon a mound. You may use the brush to remove the center area for a two-humped camel or leave well enough alone for a single-humped camel. Use the swan-neck lesson for the camel's neck. The head would be very similar to the horse's, perhaps a bit narrower. Combine the camel with palm trees and pyramids for an oasis motif.

Example of finished sheep.

A sheep can be formed by poking down four short legs and building a cumulus cloud shape over them. Build up a bit of white on the left and pour a bit of black on the background level for a black face.

IX SEALING THE FINISHED SAND PAINTING

You have at this point learned much about the art of sand painting. If you have followed the instructions carefully, you should by now be the proud owner of many intricate and creative designs. By combining various lessons into conglomerate design schemes, and by using your imagination to a degree, fine quality art work should result.

Your meticulous finished product is fragile, however. If you choose to give it away as a gift, or if you wish to sell some of your work, it must be transported. This is where a problem could arise. Careful packing is, of course, a necessity. But, accidents do happen. A sudden stop in an automobile, or an admirer who is careless enough to pick up the finished product for a closer look, could mean disaster. Then all of your hard work would be in vain.

There is, however, an answer to the problem! Available now is a type of liquid concentrate sealer that can be applied to a finished sand design and which will harden as it drys, rendering your design immovable and permanent.

The only commercially available sealer known to the writer at this time is "Terraseal." You will probably find it where you buy your sand. This is an inexpensive and valuable asset to serious-minded sand artists. The liquid is a concentrate and must be diluted before it is applied. The bottle directions recommend mixing two ounces of the concentrate with about one quart of water, resulting in a fifteen-to-one ratio of water to concentrate.

Once the solution is mixed, pour it gently over the sand design. (You can take a paper cup, poke holes in the bottom, set it on the sand surface, and fill it with solution. This method allows the sealer to slowly leak down into the design.)

When the sand is saturated (a bit of sealer should be floating on top of the design), release any trapped air bubbles by poking your knitting needle into the center area of the design. Stir it gently in a circular motion, within the center only. This will also facilitate the saturation process.

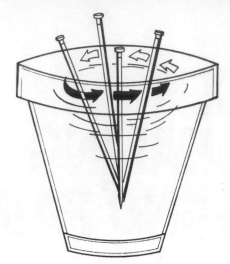

Stir in a circular motion in center area of pot.

Remove any excess sealer now with an ordinary turkey baster. Stick it down into the center area and squeeze the bulb, thus drawing out all of the extra liquid.

It will take some time for the sand painting to dry after the diluted sealer is applied, so be sure to consider this as you formulate plans for gifts or deliveries. Depending on humidity, an average pot of four and three-quarter inches will dry in forty-eight to seventy-two hours. You can, however, speed the process a bit by placing the container (sealer and sand in place) in an area where air circulation is good. (Suggestion: a sunny windowsill is acceptable.)

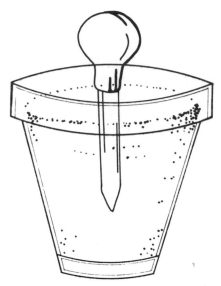

Use turkey baster to remove excess sealer.

If you wish, after the sealer is set (about an hour or two), take a teaspoon and dig out the center area of the still-wet sand. This will give you more planting room and enhance the drying process even more.

CONCLUSION

Sand art is a rewarding and profitable pastime. Your personal satisfaction is perhaps the greatest reward of all. Use these lessons to your best advantage, but above all, let imagination be your guide. Skill will come naturally with time. So do not be afraid to experiment. There is much to learn and know. There are no limitations. Enjoy!!!

Dig out center area to facilitate drying and to allow planting room.